2

Windcatcher

by AVI

D0169732

Harcourt

Orlando   Boston   Dallas   Chicago   San Diego

Visit *The Learning Site!*

www.harcourtschool.com

For David Gullette,
Commodore of Sawdy Pond

AUTHOR'S NOTE
Look at a real map of Connecticut and you will indeed see the
Thimble Islands. Windcatcher, however, is a work of fiction, and
for the sake of the story I have changed a few of the island and
surrounding area names.

This edition is published by special arrangement with Simon & Schuster Books for Young Readers, an imprint of Simon & Schuster Children's Publishing Division.

Grateful acknowledgment is made to Simon & Schuster Books for Young Readers, an imprint of Simon & Schuster Children's Publishing Division for permission to reprint *Windcatcher* by Avi. Copyright © 1991 by Avi Wortis.

Printed in the United States of America

ISBN   0-15-314377-0

2   3   4   5   6   7   8   9   10   060   03   02   01

1777

"All hands!" came the frightened cry. "All hands!"

His majesty's sailing ship Swallow heeled sharply. In Quartermaster Littlejohn's cabin, the oil lamp swung wildly, sending shadows leaping about as if in search of safety. An iron chest broke from its bonds, slid across the floor, and smashed into a table, shattering it. Bits of crockery and glass whirled through the air.

Littlejohn, asleep in his bunk, bolted up. A shrieking wind filled his ears. He found it difficult to breathe. He had to grab hold of the bedpost to keep himself from being thrown.

"All hands! All hands!"

Littlejohn, thinking the Swallow was under rebel attack, looked wildly about for the chest. The chest—with its iron straps and three locks—contained the entire payroll for General Burgoyne's Royal Army of the North. That money was Littlejohn's responsibility.

When another blow came, shaking the Swallow bow

1

to stern, *thoughts of war vanished. Littlejohn understood. They had been caught, not by rebels, but by a terrible storm.*

With an agonizing groan of splintering oak, an overhead beam thudded down, missing Littlejohn by inches. The next moment water slid in beneath the door and lapped the far wall. But as the ship heaved again, the foaming water rushed away.

Terrified—eyes wide with fright, shaved head glistening with sweat—Littlejohn staggered up. Even as he did, the Swallow *seemed to drop into a bottomless pit. The next moment she hit a rock and shuddered convulsively.*

Again the ship plunged. The iron chest leaped across the room and struck Littlejohn in the legs, tossing him into the air like a ninepin. He dropped heavily, hitting his head against a clothing box. Dizziness contorted his thoughts. The ship, swinging wildly, twisted them even more.

"She's struck!" came a desperate cry. "She's struck!"

Littlejohn tried to see where the iron chest was. He must not lose it.

As if drawn by his thoughts, the chest slid toward him. Littlejohn held up a hand. The impact of the chest sent a wrenching pain up his arm.

A banging on his cabin door. "Littlejohn!" came a shout.

"Get me out!" the quartermaster bellowed. "Get me out!"

Someone tried to get in. But the door—for security's sake—had been bolted from the inside.

The waves struck harder. The winds intensified. The ship spun, lifted, dropped.

"Boats away!" came a new cry. "Boats away!"

Littlejohn hurled himself at the door, clawing at the bolt which kept him in.

The iron chest, like a prisoner determined to punish his keeper, flew at him again, pinning him against the door. But as the ship rolled, the chest fell away, careening against the farthest wall and cracking it. Water poured in.

As the seawater rose, Littlejohn managed to slide the lock out of its catch. But when the door burst open, a wall of water rolled in, pushing him back, almost drowning him.

"Abandon ship! Abandon ship!"

It was terror that drove Littlejohn now. Choking on swallowed water, he clawed his way back to the door. The iron chest filled the doorway and blocked his way. In panic he threw himself forward. As he did one of his hands struck the oil lamp. With a hiss it plunged into the water and went out. In the roaring blackness the ship struck another rock.

* * *

By dawn the sea was calm, its surface rocking with indifferent drift. Wood bits bobbed. Shreds of sail entwined with weeds. Stretching into the distance, a multitude of islands glowed hazy and green in the morning sun.

A solitary figure, weak, broken, clothing in shreds, staggered from the water. Once on the beach, he flung himself down. Arms spread to either side, the man breathed deeply of land and life.

CHAPTER 1

"Dad," Tony Souza said, "what's money *for* if you can't spend it?" It was a Saturday, the first day of summer vacation, but to Tony his vacation already felt like a disaster.

"Keep your money in the bank," his father said. He was unloading the dish rack.

"Dad," Tony pressed, "if *you* had gotten up every morning at six for a *year*, delivered newspapers, got wet, got cold, fought off dogs, and made collections from people who didn't want to pay, you'd want to use the money *you* earned the way *you* wanted, wouldn't you?"

"Tony, people are not allowed on roads with a motor vehicle until they are fifteen. A motor scooter is a motor vehicle. You are eleven."

"Then what am I going to do with the three hundred dollars I made?"

"I gave you a suggestion."

Tony sat on the front steps. In one week, according to his parents' plan, he would go for a twenty-one-day stay at his grandma's house on the Connecticut shore. When he had been younger, it was fun to learn to swim and to sit on a beach all day. And Grandma Souza—though her English was sort of embarrassing—was all right. But *now*, Tony didn't know any kids where she lived. And he hated doing things alone. It would be a bore.

Back from Connecticut, he would go with his parents on their annual camping trip with Uncle Umberto and his family. Tony grimaced. The only thing worse than being with no kids was being with babies.

That would leave only two weeks before school began. *Some* vacation.

Tony stuck his head inside the house. "I'm going over to Jamal's!" he shouted.

When Tony slumped up Jamal's driveway, Rick, Jamal's older brother, was working on the red motorbike. Jamal was there, too.

"They going to let you buy it?" Jamal called.

Tony shook his head.

"Too bad," Rick said. "This baby isn't going to last long. Got two calls this morning from my newspaper ad."

Tony wandered back down to the street.

Jamal ran after him. "What are you going to do with that money?"

"I'll think of something."

"What happens if your parents change their minds?"

"They won't."

"Want to watch TV?" Jamal suggested. "Play ball? Should be some guys at the park."

Tony hesitated. The thought of being with friends was tempting. But spending his money was urgent. "Later," he said. Shoving his hands in his pockets, he set off.

First he went into a bicycle shop. Then a sports shop. After that it was a toy store that carried computer games. Then there was the Mart. As Tony wandered up and down the long aisles, everything seemed like junk.

Then he saw it. It was a sailboat—no more than twelve feet in length—hanging from the ceiling. Made of some plasticlike stuff, its outside was blue, its inside white. A wooden rudder was at the back. The mast was metal. The sail bore red letters which proclaimed the boat's name: *Snark*. A large price tag dangled from the hull.

SALE!
$295.00

The moment Tony saw the boat, he knew, sure as he knew anything, what he wanted, what he needed, was a Snark.

He ran home and poured out the news of his discovery, telling his parents all the ways the sailboat would make his summer exciting.

When Tony saw them give each other a look, he knew it was not out of the question. He pressed harder, insisting they go to the store right away.

At the Mart, his mother gazed up at the boat and said, "It's like a polystyrene cup with a sail."

"Ma, it's a *sailboat*! Can I get it?"

"There are some things to check first," his mother returned. "Come on. I have a friend who sails."

"Ma . . . !" Tony wailed again.

"Tony, it's not sailing anywhere."

Once home, Tony's mother called her friend and asked for a reaction to a Snark.

"You can't cross oceans with it," said the friend, "or handle bad weather, but in protected areas it'll do fine. In fact, it's just about perfect for a kid who wants to learn to sail. And you can't beat the price."

When Tony heard the report he did a cartwheel in the dining room, narrowly missing a lamp.

"Cool it!" his father cautioned. "Your mom and I need some privacy to discuss this."

Told to leave the room while they talked, Tony tried to listen through the door to what they were saying. He did hear his father make a call. Speak to someone. Hang up. Then Tony was called back into the room.

"The answer," his mother said, "is yes. . . ."

"If . . ." his father put in quickly, cutting off Tony's cheer, *"if* certain conditions are met."

"I agree to everything," Tony said.

"We called your grandma for her approval."

"And . . . ?"

His parents exchanged looks. "She said yes," his father said.

"All right!" Tony called.

"Second condition!" his mother said hastily. "We'll pay, but you *must* have sailing lessons."

"No problem."

"Finally," his father added, "you have to promise— really promise—that whenever you sail, you'll wear a life jacket."

"Dad," Tony pleaded, "I just said, I agree to *everything.*"

Monday morning Tony and his mother went to the bank, withdrew his newspaper money, and headed for the Mart. Heart thumping, Tony counted out fifteen crisp, new twenty-dollar bills onto the counter.

"Plus eighteen dollars tax," the salesperson said.

Tony's heart sank. He looked up at his mother. She looked at him.

"I'll clean the car," Tony said. "And wax it. Three times."

"I would have paid anyway," she said with a laugh. "But that's a deal." She also purchased a life jacket.

Store people loaded the box with the *Snark* atop the

car. Once home, Tony spent the day—as he had promised—trying not to open the box. But by eight o'clock that night, with his parent's help, the *Snark* was assembled. She looked cool, if crowded, in the middle of their living room, with her white and blue sail hoisted on the seven-foot mast.

"Wait a minute," Tony said, "what's a Snark?"

"Look it up," his mother suggested.

In the dictionary he read:

Snark: A mysterious, imaginary animal.

CHAPTER 2

"Can I go sailing soon as we get there?" Tony wanted to know.

His father laughed. "You have to learn first."

It was Saturday morning. The *Snark* was tied to the top of the car. Tony and his father were speeding west along the interstate. Traffic was heavy under a sky that was turning darker by the moment. From his seat, Tony could see the bow extending over the windshield. In his lap lay a history of sailing ships that his mother had given him as a going-away present. But for most of the trip Tony searched for water. Now and again he caught glimpses of Long Island Sound.

As they got off the interstate it started to rain, a cloudburst. They moved slowly now as they went past the town of Guilford. Then they swung back west on Route 146 before going over the Chaffinch River.

As suddenly as the rain had come, it stopped. It poured sunlight now. Tree leaves seemed to drip emerald green. The black asphalt road steamed. A heavy smell of sea filled the air.

Swallows Bay was on a peninsula with two points spread in fishtail fashion. The western side was called Joshua Point. The east side was Haycock Point. Between the two lay Swallows Bay Harbor.

Down both points ran two rows of houses. None were new. All were white or gray with shingle roofs. Most had porches with trellises through which flowers curled.

As always—a Souza ritual—they drove past Grandma's house, down to the tip of Haycock Point. There they stopped.

At the end was a gravel circle for turning around. In the middle of the circle stood a statue of Captain Ezra Littlejohn, the portly founder of the town. He seemed to be staring out into the sound and sky as if waiting for something to appear. The Souza family joke was that—considering the captain's belly—he was waiting for his dinner.

To the right of the road was Carluci's Fish Store and a wooden dock which extended fifty yards into the harbor. A good number of boats were tied to it. More boats were in the harbor. There was also a public access ramp for people to run their boat trailers directly into the water.

To Tony, the sound always seemed as big as an ocean. On clear days you could see twelve miles, across to Long Island. As he gazed across, he saw the rainstorm scudding across the water. It was like a curtain being pulled away.

When Mr. Souza swung the car around, Tony read the inscription on the statue's base.

FOUNDER OF THE TOWN OF SWALLOWS BAY
CAPTAIN EZRA LITTLEJOHN
b. 1731—d. 1821

"1731," Tony said. "Wasn't that before America?"

"Before the United States of America," his father replied as they drove up the road.

Grandma Souza was a short, wide woman. Her broad face and bright, dark eyes were framed by jet black hair. Though she wore nothing but somber dresses, it was rare for Tony to see her without a smile. That moment was no exception. "Here he is!" she cried when she saw him. "Bravo! The new sailor!"

Hardly did Tony leap from the car than she wrapped her arms around him and gave him an engulfing hug.

Tony grinned with delight.

Grandma's house was a small, two-story frame building, both cheerful and bright. The furniture was all white wicker and wood. Pink curtains graced the windows. On a wall over an old upright piano, a map of the area had been placed. Multicolored silk flowers nodded among ceramic shepherds. The air was sweet

13

with lemon, a sure promise of *supiros*, the meringue cookies Grandma made.

Tony lugged his suitcase up the steps to the second floor. By tradition his room was off to the left. When he entered, the first thing he saw was a ship model on the dresser.

Mounted on a small stand, the ship had three square sails on each of three masts. The sails were yellow with age, the rigging complicated. Eight miniature cannons, four to each side, poked through gunports. On her stern hung a British flag.

Tony tore down the steps. "Grandma! Where did that ship model come from?"

"Something your grandfather got."

"Must have cost a fortune."

She shrugged. "It was stored. But now, I think you like her."

As they sat down for lunch Tony asked, "When can I start sailing lessons?"

"Everything's fixed," Grandma announced. "Chris, from the Carluci family—the fish store people—will do it."

"How much?"

"Tony!" his father cried.

"I said to them," Grandma went on, " 'Mr. Carluci, Tony is a good swimmer.' Right?"

"Got my junior Red Cross swimming card at the Y," Tony said.

"Came in second in the fifty-meter freestyle for his age class," his father added proudly.

"Won five bucks," Tony bragged.

"And he'll always wear his life jacket."

"Can I start soon?" Tony wanted to know.

"If you like, this afternoon."

As soon as lunch was over, Tony rushed outside. Standing in front of his grandma's house, he could look down the two hundred yards of low hill road to the harbor. Boats, most of them brilliant white, rode easily upon glistening blue-green water.

With a burst of excitement, Tony ran all the way to Carluci's Fish Store. There was sawdust on the floor. A fat orange cat slept in a nest of nets. Behind the glass-faced counter were trays of fish, clams, and mussels embedded in crushed ice. A young man stood behind the counter. Another man—looking like an older brother—was sitting on a stool.

"Can I help you?" the one behind the counter asked.

Tony asked, "Is Chris here?"

"Sure is," said the older one. "Out back. You the Souza boy?"

Tony nodded yes.

"Hi. Go on out around the store, onto the dock. Pumping gas. Can't miss."

At the end of the dock, working the gas pump, was a teenage girl dressed in faded jeans, rubber boots, and a T-shirt that read, "Fish Is Brain Food."

Tony, suddenly shy, glanced into the motorboat that was getting gas. A young man and woman were in her. They had digging equipment—shovels, picks, some buckets.

The girl on the dock finished pumping, then collected the money. As the people in the boat pushed off, she watched them go before turning to Tony. "Hi. Help you with something?"

"I'm looking for Chris."

"That's me, Christina," said the girl with a big smile and a welcome hand. "You Tony Souza?"

Tony nodded. He couldn't take his eyes off the speedboat that was roaring out of the harbor.

"Ready to learn sailing?" Chris asked.

"I'd like to."

"Not as fast as those folks," she said with a nod toward the now-disappearing speedboat. "But a lot more fun."

"Where they going so fast?"

"Those folks?" Chris shrugged. "They're looking for the treasure."

"What treasure?"

"The Swallows Bay treasure."

Tony looked at Chris with surprise.

She laughed. "Forget it. It's only a legend. What I want to know is, when are we going to have your first lesson?"

CHAPTER 3

Tony and his father lifted the *Snark* off the car roof and lowered it into the water. The mast was quickly put up. The sail was hoisted. The little boat, rocking gently, sat neat as a duck. Tony glowed with pleasure.

Chris, wearing her own life jacket, came up. She introduced herself to Tony's father.

"Now Tony," Grandma said. *"Boa viagem*—have a good trip!"* She and Tony's father drove off.

Tony, suddenly anxious, watched them go. He turned to Chris. "Guess I'm ready."

"Don't worry," Chris said as if reading his mind. "You'll do fine."

Chris began with the basics. She explained the words sailors used, everything from "port," the left side of the boat when facing toward the bow, to "tack," the way you move against the wind.

There were terms like "dagger board"—the blade-like piece of plywood which would allow the boat to sail against the wind; "tiller" (the stick attached to the rudder); "reach"—sailing across the wind; and "luff"—to turn into the wind. With each word, Chris explained something about sailing.

Tony was starting to get dizzy when Chris said, "Enough talk. Time to do it."

First she told Tony to sit forward next to the dagger board. Then she waded into the water, gave them a push, and jumped into the stern. Immediately, one of her hands went to the tiller. The other hand grabbed the sheet, the rope tied to the boom. The boom kept the sail stiff at the bottom.

"Drop the dagger board!" she called.

Tony shoved the dagger board down through the centerboard case.

With what looked to Tony like effortless ease, Chris cut through Swallows Bay Harbor and the maze of moored boats. Then she tacked back around Joshua Point into the place known as Joshua Cove.

There she showed Tony a variety of maneuvers: turning, ways to go faster and slower, even how to come to a relatively quick stop if necessary by turning into the wind.

"Okay," Chris said. "Time to trade places."

"Now?" Tony replied with surprise.

"Hey, it's your boat."

Staying low, Tony moved toward the stern of the boat on the starboard side. Chris, on the port side, moved toward the bow. As they shifted, the boat rocked, making Tony uneasy.

Seated in the stern, Tony placed one hand on the tiller. He put the other on the sheet just as he had seen Chris do.

"Now," Chris said, "we don't want to get out of the cove, okay? You've got a way to go before that. Stay clear of that tidal flat there. Now, see that little island?" she said, pointing to what looked like a pile of rocks.

Tony nodded. "What about it?"

"It's called Horse Island. There are lots of submerged rocks in front of it. So make sure you keep away. Lots of rocks around here. You've got to learn all the danger places."

Heart beating fast, Tony shifted the tiller. The boat swung about.

"Pull on the sheet," Chris called.

Tony pulled. The sail stiffened, then filled. They began to pick up speed. He felt tension in his arm. All of a sudden the boat was slipping forward with what felt like no effort, beating the waves with a steady rhythm, running with the wind. A rush of excitement filled Tony. *He was sailing.*

Tony watched over the bow of the boat. They were moving toward Horse Island fast.

"Steer between the islands," Chris cautioned. "That one there is called Foskett."

Tony made an adjustment. "Like this?" he asked.

"Right. Now, soon as you get past Foskett, bring her about."

"Which way?"

"Port."

Excited, Tony pulled the tiller hard. The *Snark* veered sharply, straight for Foskett Island. The next moment there was a wrenching jolt.

"Rocks!" Chris cried. "Turn to starboard!"

Tony, trying to remember which way Chris meant, gave the tiller a yank. The boat slipped from the rocks. As they sailed between the islands, the *Snark* began rapidly picking up speed. Now they were heading right for the shore, getting closer every moment.

"Bring her about!" Chris shouted suddenly.

Nervous from his last mistake, Tony pushed the tiller.

"The other way!" Chris cried.

Tony did. Too much. The boom swung wildly. Trying to adjust, Tony jerked the tiller back. The *Snark* swung sharply, heeling hard. The mast careened. Tony, frightened, let go of everything. The next second the boat capsized.

CHAPTER 4

As Tony hit the water he lost his breath. Struggling, he began to sink. Even as he did he felt the upward pull of his life jacket. Spitting, flailing arms and legs, he broke through to the water's surface.

"Let your jacket hold you!" he heard Chris shout. "Don't fight! Get your breath!"

Tony stopped thrashing. And when he realized the jacket would hold him, he relaxed. With circular motions of his arms he turned himself about in search of Chris.

"Over here!" she called.

Tony turned again. Chris was standing up, waist deep, laughing. "Think I'd try you out in deep water?" Chris asked. "It's only four feet deep."

Cautiously, Tony let his legs down. To his surprise, he touched bottom. Realizing how funny he must look, he stood up. He felt his face get hot.

"Seriously," Chris said, "good sailing is as much

safety as it's anything. Don't ever let anyone tease you from thinking otherwise. Besides, capsizing like that is good. Now it doesn't scare you. Believe me, it's going to happen."

Tony waded over to where the *Snark* lay, mast and sail flat on the water.

Chris got Tony to reach over and grasp the boat's side while putting his foot onto the dagger board. As he pressed the dagger board down, the boat, still full of water, righted herself. She sat like a full bathtub in the middle of a lake.

"See," Chris said, "this kind of boat can't sink."

Tony, following instructions, lowered the sail. Then he began to splash water out. Chris worked, too. An hour later, with Tony at the tiller, the boat crunched softly onto the landing ramp.

Chris showed Tony how to get the mast down, roll the sail, and tie everything up. They put the boat underneath the dock, tying it securely.

"Won't anyone take it?" Tony worried out loud.

"You're in Swallows Bay Harbor," Chris said. "People don't steal."

They walked up the landing ramp. "Tony," she assured him, "you're going to be terrific."

"Seems hard."

"It's mostly practice. Honest. Remember, my family and I have been messing around boats all our lives.

My father and one brother are fishermen. My mother teaches marine biology at the high school. And Steve, my other brother, he's harbor master."

"What's that?"

"Sort of like a water cop."

"What about you?"

"Don't know yet. Sometimes I think I'd like to be a boat designer."

"Are you going sailing with me again?"

"Oh, sure. A few more times. Come by tomorrow, and we'll set a time. Really," she said, with a final wave, "you're going to do great."

Tony, feeling somewhat more confident, watched her go. He wished he had messed around boats all *his* life.

As Tony came across the road, he stopped to look up at the statue of Captain Littlejohn. The metal statue, dark with age, mounted on a large rock, was life-sized. The face was solemn, staring.

The captain wore what Tony supposed was the uniform of olden days: buckled shoes, wide trousers over long stockings, a long-tailed jacket with cuffs, hair tied behind. One arm was bent across his chest; the other was straight down. In that hand was a spyglass.

Tony had looked at that statue a thousand times before. This time he studied it with new interest, trying to figure out what kind of person Captain Littlejohn was and what kind of ships he had commanded. Tony wondered what it would be like to know what the real Captain Littlejohn knew, every one of his secrets.

"How come," Tony said during dinner that night, "this town isn't called Littlejohn Bay instead of Swallows Bay?"

"Probably lots of swallows around," his father offered.

Grandma nodded. "Or, maybe it's like the land, a tail of a swallow." She got up, went into the living room, and came back with a booklet.

"Something the newspaper gave at the bicentennial," she explained. "Tells all the histories of the towns around here."

Tony found one small paragraph.

SWALLOWS BAY

Founded around 1783 following the Revolution. Was a fishing port for many years and has since become a summer community, though some commercial fishing is still done. Historic statue of Captain Ezra Littlejohn, the traditional founder, was set up by his widow in 1822. The area, and Littlejohn, have long been associated with a tradition of buried treasure, though no proof of its existence has ever been found.

"Doesn't say why it's called Swallows Bay," Tony said. "Does talk about a treasure."

Grandma sniffed. "That's, you know, to give summer tourists a thing to do."

"I saw people going out looking for it today," Tony told her.

"Hey," his father cried, bopping Tony on the arm, "go for it. Beats delivering newspapers. Mama, this boy *loves* money."

Tony acknowledged the truth with a grin.

In bed that night, Tony began to read the book about old sailing ships that his mother had given him. It started with a picture of an ancient Egyptian boat and ended with the *Eagle*, one of the sailing ships—the ones called tall ships—that modern navies use for training.

As Tony went through the book, he came upon a chapter which told about the finding of sunken ships. It included photos of ancient wrecks taken with underwater cameras. The pictures revealed dim outlines of partially buried timbers. To Tony the images looked more like the bones of huge fish than the remains of old ships.

Tony was still reading when Grandma came up and sat on his bed. "Tony," she said, "I'm happy you come to stay a little. You won't get unhappy with me, will you?"

Tony assured her he would not.

"Good. Now what's that you read?"

He showed her the book.

"Your grandfather, he loved those kinds of books."

Tony didn't remember his grandfather. He had died when Tony was two. "Where did he get that ship?" he asked, nodding at the model on the dresser.

"I think," Grandma said, "he found it in a yard sale. Maybe this book tells what kind it is. Tony, you know, Portuguese people are always fine sailors."

"They are?"

"Oh, sure. Vasco da Gama. Henry the Navigator. So, you'll be one, too." She bent over, kissed his forehead, then whispered, *"Espero que vece alcance vento dos seus desejos."*

"What's that mean?"

"It's Portuguese sailors' talk. 'May you catch the wind you want.' "

"How do you say 'sailor'?"

"Marinheiro."

"Marinheiro," Tony repeated. " 'Sailboat'?"

"O barco a vela."

"O barco a vela."

Grandma smiled broadly. "Bravo!" she cried, and kissed him good-night.

After Grandma left, Tony slipped out of bed and went to examine the model close up. With care, he lifted it off its stand and turned it around. On the ship's stern, on what the book called the sterncastle, were some letters. Though they were smudged and difficult to read, he could make out an *S*, an *L*, finally a *W*. For a moment he stared at them. Then he understood. The ship's name was the *Swallow*.

CHAPTER 5

Next morning, as soon as breakfast was over, Tony ran down to Carluci's. Chris was busy with customers. When she saw Tony, she called out, "Ready for another dunking?"

Tony, grinning, nodded yes.

"How about two-thirty?" Chris said, plopping a plump bluefish on the scale.

When Tony went back up the hill, he again looked at the statue of Captain Littlejohn. The statue was dark with age, almost black. But the spyglass in the figure's hand was green.

Curious, Tony drew closer. After a few moments of study, he realized that whoever made the statue had placed what must have been a *real* spyglass in the figure's hand. Tony was puzzled at first, but then he figured that there must have been no point in modeling a spyglass if a real one was available.

He climbed onto the statue's pedestal for a closer

examination. Yes, the spyglass was real. It was just that the tube appeared to be packed with dirt.

Tony looked up at the statue's face. The captain's stare was so intent that Tony found himself turning to see what the eyes of the statue were focused on.

What he saw was the motorboat Chris had pointed out to him the day before, the one with the people digging for treasure. The same young man and woman were in her.

As Tony watched, they took off at top speed out of the harbor. Once past Joshua Point, they were quickly out of sight. Tony, wondering where they were going, headed home. There he found his father ready to leave. He was hoping to beat bad traffic. "By the time we come get you," Mr. Souza said to Tony, "I expect you to be commodore of the Swallows Bay Fleet." He saluted smartly, making Tony laugh.

As his father's car disappeared over the hill, Grandma, standing by Tony's side, said, "All right. Time to get going."

"Where?"

"To get clams. Get your swim things on."

Grandma—still wearing her black dress—drove her old Ford up Colonial Road, cut over to Pump Lane for half a mile, then pulled up to the side of the road and stopped. They were at the far end of Joshua Cove at a marshy tidal flat. Part of the area was covered with spiky eelgrass. The rest was nothing but black sand.

Tony fetched the long-handled shovel and the bucket. Then he followed Grandma—now barefoot— to the black sand. As she turned the sand over with the long-handled shovel, Tony, at her feet, went through the muck. Every time he found a clam he held it up so she could see if it was big enough. Small ones were returned to the sand.

Grandma said, "You like to eat one?"

"*Raw?*"

"Sure. They're good that way." She took up two clams and cracked them together hard. Their shells split, exposing pale orange meat. "Here," she said, offering one to Tony. "*Ameijoas.* Clams. Try."

Tony, disgusted, shook his head. But Grandma pulled out the clam and put it in her mouth.

"Is it really good?" he asked her.

"Delicious."

"I'll eat them when they're cooked," he told her.

As they worked, Tony said, "Grandma . . ."

"What?"

"I saw those people who are looking for that treasure again."

"So?"

"They were heading out with their digging stuff. Do you think there could be a treasure?"

Grandma paused in her work to smile at Tony. "You have money on your mind all the time, don't you?"

"Nothing wrong with that, is there?"

"I don't know. But I will tell you what I do think."

"What?"

"We should put our heads together and find that treasure."

"Thought you didn't believe there was one."

"Maybe yes. Maybe no. But maybe it's a good thing to do when you're here. Think about it."

At two-thirty that afternoon, Chris appeared at the dock. She was carrying what looked like a plastic gallon milk container cut to the shape of a scoop.

"Boat bailer," she explained. "Faster than hands." She tied a string from its handle to one of the *Snark*'s cleats midships. Then she got into the bow of the boat. "Okay," she said, "it's all yours."

"From the start?" Tony said, surprised.

"Only way to learn."

Tony dropped the dagger board into its slot. Then he made sure he had the sheet ready at hand. When that was set, he pushed the *Snark* farther into the water, ready to jump in.

"Hold it!" Chris called.

Tony stopped.

"Check the wind," Chris said. She pointed at the telltale ribbon stuck atop the mast. "Like that old song says, you can't go anywhere 'less you know which way the wind is blowing. Here's the best advice I can give you: Respect the wind. It's stronger than you."

"Even when you're a good sailor?"

"It's the only way to be one."

Moments later, with Tony holding the tiller, they were on their way, cutting swiftly across the harbor, heading out on a starboard tack. Chris gave a thumbs-up sign.

Tony, feeling more and more confident, called, "Which way?"

"Joshua Cove. Best place to practice."

Which is exactly what Tony did, going back and forth, turning, slowing, even coming to a stop—luffing—whatever Chris told him to do. He did make mistakes. He got mixed up. Still, he knew he was doing things more and more smoothly.

After an hour, Chris called, "Ready to head out some?"

"Sure."

"Okay. Aim for that point of land. Sachem Head. Just stay wide of the rocks there."

Tony shifted the tiller, tacking to port. For a while they sailed that way. "What does Sachem Head mean?" he asked.

"*Sachem*'s an Indian word," Chris explained. "All the names around here come from things that happened a long time ago. It's like a book, if you know how to read it."

"What about Swallows Bay?"

"Somebody must have bitten off more than they could chew," Chris suggested.

They were in the sound now, the *Snark* slapping the chop with a regular beat. "Now to Clark's Point," Chris suggested. She pointed the way.

Tony did it easily.

After a while Chris called, "Okay! Time for home. Bring her about."

Tony swung the tiller, ducking as the boom shifted. The *Snark* turned gracefully. As they turned, Tony got a good look at a long string of islands that lay about a mile and a half southwest along the coast. There were many of them, mostly small. "What are they?" he asked.

"The Thimble Islands," Chris explained. "About thirty and all different. Sort of a mile-long chain from Harrison Point. Some are real small, not much bigger than a pile of rocks. Others are about a thousand feet wide. The big ones are crowded with trees. A couple have fishermen's shacks on them."

"Can you sail there?" Tony wanted to know.

Chris shook her head. "Got to be careful. The water and currents around there are crazy. There's a forty-foot drop off Dogfish Island. At Outer Island it's only three feet deep, but the current is like a river. Then, when you get to Cut-in-Two Island, it all depends on the tide.

"And there are lots of rocks. Some you can see. Others are just above the water. If the tide is right, the only hint that those rocks are there is a ripple of water on the surface, if that. Not safe. Get the idea?"

"I suppose. Those names for real?"

"On the maps. But as soon as you get to know it all, a big storm comes in—like that hurricane we had last fall—and things get all turned round."

"What do you mean?"

"Where it used to be shallow, sand gets stripped and the place becomes deep. Or, worse, what was a deep channel, silts up shallow."

"That fast?"

"Overnight."

"Awesome."

"Don't worry. We aren't in hurricane season."

"Hope not."

"Okay, skipper, head for home!" Chris shouted.

"Aye, aye, sir!" Tony called with another pull on the tiller.

Leaving behind a gurgling wake, the *Snark* cut through the water effortlessly. Tony, with one hand on the sheet to keep the sail from blowing out, the other hand on the tiller, felt as if his whole body were humming. The silence sang. With a salt wind blowing in his face, he felt as if he could go on forever.

"I love this!" he yelled.

Chris flashed a thumbs-up sign.

CHAPTER 6

That night, after a clam chowder dinner and homemade bread, Grandma said, "Now, we can do some different things. Play some games. Read. Watch TV. Do nothing. Or talk about treasure."

Tony looked at her suspiciously. "You really think I could find it?"

"Sure."

"People don't believe in it, you know."

"You said you watched people go looking."

"That's what Chris said."

"Well then, if they look, you look, too."

Tony thought for a moment. "Yeah, but you have to know something about it first. A clue."

"We do."

"What?"

"That little book." Grandma got the bicentennial booklet from the living room. Tony read the section on Swallows Bay again.

"I don't think it says anything," he said, handing it over.

Grandma adjusted her reading glasses, read the paragraph, then said, "It says the treasure was buried, and that it has something to do with this Littlejohn, the one who found the town."

"The statue guy."

"I look at his face and do you know what I think?"

"No."

"That he's trying to remember something."

"We could ask him."

Grandma laughed. "But I think you're right. We need to know more about *Capitano* Littlejohn."

"You're serious, aren't you?"

Grandma looked slyly at Tony. "Ah, Tony. All that *ouro*."

"*Ouro?*"

"Gold. It would be fun to find, wouldn't it?"

"Like winning the lottery," he agreed gleefully.

The next morning was not nearly as bright as the day before. There were high clouds in the west. At breakfast, Grandma said, "What time have you your lesson?"

"Three."

"Better go and ask Chris if she can make the lesson sooner. I think there's rain this afternoon."

Tony did check, and Chris, agreeing with Grandma,

set an earlier lesson time. Tony started off.

"Yo, Tony!" Chris called after him. "Bring weather gear. Maybe you can get a little rough water experience. You'll need it sailing around here."

They set off at about ten-thirty. The sky was grayer than before. A sharp breeze blew. Tony was glad he had on a nylon windbreaker under his life jacket.

Chris looked out over the harbor into the sound. "I don't think we should go too far," she said. "Your boat can't take anything stronger than this. Not made for it. Too risky. But a good stiff wind will give you practice. During summer, nine out of ten times, the wind comes from the south. Not today. Let's go."

The *Snark* shot out of the harbor, spanking the white-capped waves. A constant spray brought chilly water into the boat.

Chris, while keeping a close eye on what Tony was doing, bailed steadily.

Tony was a little nervous about the weather but sensed the challenge of it. Holding both sheet and tiller tightly, he felt the boat straining against wind and waves. As the wind blew gusts, the aluminum mast bent like a bow.

"Stay over by Joshua Cove," Chris called. "Weather's coming on faster than I thought it would."

Tony brought them about sharply. With the wind at their backs, the *Snark* seemed to leap forward.

She pulled so hard that more than once Tony almost lost the sail. To keep it from slipping, he wrapped the sheet tightly around his hand.

Chris kept glancing at the thickening sky. "Take her around Foskett, along Sachem Head. Then back. That'll be enough."

Tony did as he was told, trying to thread his way through the two little islands.

"Don't forget the rocks off Horse!" Chris shouted.

Tony, seeing foaming waves breaking hard against Horse Island, nodded. He wanted nothing to do with them or the rocks he couldn't see. He eased a bit to starboard.

"Good . . . good," Chris called encouragingly. Then she cried, "Ready to bring her about!"

"Ready!" Tony echoed.

"Now!" Chris hollered, faster than Tony thought she would.

Taken by surprise, Tony pulled the tiller. As the boat turned, the unrestrained boom swept so fast across the *Snark* that it pulled the sheet out of Tony's hand. He lunged for it but missed. With nothing holding it back, the sail swept full circle and wrapped around the mast. The swing of the sail and the sudden shift of weight proved too much. Over they went. Capsized.

CHAPTER 7

Practice from the other day paid off. Tony let the life jacket hold him up in the rough water. Cautiously, he stretched his feet, found the bottom, shook his head clear, and looked for the *Snark*. Chris, already standing, was working to right the boat. Tony waded over. "Sorry!" he said.

"It's all experience," Chris insisted. "Let's see you get her up quick, though."

The *Snark* was afloat in minutes. Together, too, they worked to untangle the sail.

"Better to tie the sheet to the tiller," Chris said, doing it. "I should have suggested that."

Rain began.

"Can you take her in?" Chris asked.

"I think so."

"Come on," she said, a note of concern shading her voice. "We need to move."

After bailing as fast as possible, they scrambled over the gunnels and took their places.

"Let's go!" Chris called. With the sail wet and heavy, the *Snark* moved sluggishly. By the time they reached land, they were soaked and cold.

Chris started to take down the mast.

"Wouldn't it be better to keep the sail up and let it dry out?" Tony asked.

Chris shook her head. "A wind can always catch a full sail, shred it, and pull your boat apart—take her so far you'll never see her again. It's a lot easier to take the time and do it right. She can always dry out later."

With the boat safely stowed under the dock, Chris said, "Let's get something warm to drink."

In the back of the fish store, Chris threw Tony a towel, while Steve, her older brother—the harbor master who had laughed to see them enter so bedraggled—set down some hot cider. It warmed them quickly.

"You did fine," Chris said, making Tony feel better. "How you feeling?"

"Good."

"You know, I think you can handle your boat alone. Honest. The rest is mostly practice. Just make sure to stay close in for a while. You know, around Joshua Cove until you feel really comfortable. And always play it safe."

Tony wasn't sure what to say.

"Anyway, I've got stuff to do tomorrow. How about you going out alone tomorrow? Then, day after, I'll go with you again."

"Sure."

"Want me to speak to your grandma?"

"I think you better."

The two of them sat in the store for a while getting warmed up. Tony recalled something he wanted to ask Chris.

"Remember you telling me about those people who were looking for treasure?"

"What about them?"

"Do you think there really *is* a treasure?"

Chris shrugged. "Some folks do." She grinned and turned to her brother. "Do you?"

"Wish there was," Steve answered. "Where were those people looking?" he wondered.

"Didn't see," Chris told him. "They were only talking about it. Down the coast some place. From the look of their tools they were digging. Next time they come in, I'll ask."

"Actually," her brother said, "it's illegal to salvage sea wrecks or treasure in the water without the state's permission." He turned to Tony. "Thinking of looking?" he asked.

Tony nodded sheepishly.

"You won't be the first," Chris said. "Or the last."

"Just remember," the harbor master put in, "if you find it—it belongs to the state of Connecticut."

"*All* of it?"

"That's the law."

"Look what a cat dragged in," Grandma exclaimed when Tony came into the house from a pouring rain. "You dry off and put on warm things. I'll get lunch on the table. Then you'll tell me your adventures."

Over hot soup, sandwiches, and cookies, Tony told Grandma how he and Chris had gotten caught in the storm.

"Lucky it was not the hurricane that came last fall."

"Was it real bad?"

"Oh, sure. It blow like crazy. Make the house shake. And, with the full moon, the tides were super high. All the men who dig clams were upset."

"Why?"

"Well, everywhere, beaches and bottoms shifted. Changed everything. They had to find the clam beds all over again."

"Wow," Tony said. "Wish I could have seen that."

Grandma sighed. "I think you have the spirit of the old sailors. Tony, I do love it that you sail, but, it would not be me if I did not worry."

"Grandma, Chris said I could sail on my own."

"Oh?"

"She said she'd call you."

For a moment Grandma said nothing. Then she said, "Well, the more you learn with Chris, the better I like it. Now then," she continued, changing the subject, "we've got to go out."

"Where?"

"We are going to get that treasure, aren't we?"

"Now? In the rain?"

"In the library."

"There's no treasure there."

"That's the little you know," she snorted.

"Guess what?" Tony said as he got on his coat. "Even if I found it I couldn't keep it. That's what Chris's brother said."

"Does that mean you don't want to look?"

"Be a lot of work for nothing."

"Yes or no?"

"I suppose. . . ."

The Guilford library was more like an old mansion than the kind of city library Tony knew. A glittering chandelier hung from the ceiling. Old paintings were on the walls. Bookcases were made of wood. Only the books looked new.

Grandma chatted with the librarian behind the information desk. Then, after Tony was introduced,

Grandma explained what they were looking for. "It's something about our statue, that Captain Littlejohn. The one who began Swallows Bay."

The librarian thought for a moment, then said, "I think we have something on him in the vertical file." He led them down an aisle to a file cabinet, pulled it open, ran his fingers over the folders, and plucked one out. "Try this," he said.

The folder contained newspaper stories. A couple had pictures of the statue.

"Now then," Grandma said to Tony, "you read and I'll read."

After reading, they compared what they had learned. The few facts were:

That nothing was or is known about Littlejohn's place of birth or where he came from. Some question if he even really was a captain.

It is known that shortly after the American Revolution, he settled in what became Swallows Bay, which until that time was uninhabited.

Littlejohn named the harbor Swallows Bay.

Littlejohn lived out his days there.

Littlejohn was not considered a very successful merchant.

Littlejohn was known as an eccentric who spent many hours trudging the shores near the Swallows Bay area in search of treasure which he never found. He was quoted as saying it was his duty to find it.

Littlejohn left a will specifying that a statue of himself be placed in its present locale, going so far as having it designed before his death in 1821.

It was his widow who set up the statue.

"I don't think this helps much," Tony said.

"He's full of secrets," Grandma agreed. "Before he came to Swallows Bay, *nada*. Nothing. Even after he didn't do so good. A little bit like your grandfather and me when we came here."

"But you weren't here then," Tony reminded her.

"Certainly no!" Grandma said with a snort. "And we came because your grandfather wasn't well. But Tony, we came because he liked it. In those days, it was cheap. You see, we had reasons. That's the way with most people. But, if there was no one here—that is what it says—why did this Littlejohn come here?"

"Think it was the treasure?"

"Makes me think. . . ."

"But we don't know for sure."

"That's what you've got to find out. Right?"

"Right."

"Go get some books to read. You can use my card."

Tony went right to the section of books about old ships.

CHAPTER 8

Wednesday morning came up bright, brisk, and clear. Tony charged downstairs, life jacket on. Grandma was setting out breakfast.

"Solo time," Tony announced.

Grandma looked at him thoughtfully. "I did speak to Chris and yes, she did say you could go out alone."

"Can I?"

Grandma frowned. Tony watched her anxiously. Then she said, "Tony, we'll make an agreement. This first time you go out alone I want you to stay close. Do we understand that?"

"Okay."

"Then, after one hour, I'll go to the end of the dock. You can come by and show me you didn't drown."

"I'll be fine. You don't have to worry."

"That's our agreement," Grandma said firmly.

Tony ate a hurried breakfast, then ran down to the dock. There he hauled the *Snark* out and hoisted the mast and sail. He was about to jump in when he remembered the other things he was supposed to do: tie the sheet to the tiller, check the telltale, as well as make sure the bailer was there.

Now Tony worked slowly, calmly. He made sure everything was in order.

When he was ready, Tony dropped the dagger board, pointed the *Snark*'s bow, pushed her out, jumped in, and hauled back on the sheet. Immediately jibing, he cut along the breeze. It was all a bit clumsy. But to his relief, the boat moved. There was one big difference. Without Chris's weight, the *Snark* moved much faster. At first it scared Tony. He was actually glad he had promised to return in an hour. That way he wouldn't be tempted to go too far.

During the hour, Tony did what he was supposed to do—sailed back and forth, practicing all the things Chris had taught him. Bit by bit his confidence grew.

At the end of the hour, he sailed back to the harbor. Grandma was nervously pacing the end of the dock. As soon as she saw Tony, she brightened and gaily waved a white handkerchief as he went by.

Tony returned a big grin.

"Come back for lunch!" she called.

"Okay!"

Tony swung around and brought his attention back to the harbor. As he did he noticed that the couple looking for the treasure was also there. They were getting their motorboat ready. Right off it occurred to Tony that he might be able to see where they were headed. *That* would be something worth bringing home for lunch.

Waiting for the couple, he tacked back and forth at the mouth of the harbor. When they came, their motorboat burst out loud and clear, leaving curls of pearly white foam. Tony cut away quickly, trying to avoid the heavy wash of waves. When he saw where the couple was heading—not out into the sound, but down the coast—he turned in pursuit.

Tony knew there was no way he could match their speed. He could only follow and watch from an increasing distance. But that he did. He saw them go right across—almost in a straight line—from Joshua Point to what Tony remembered as Clark's Point. Instead of landing as he thought they might, he saw them veer off and go past Harrison Point, then move among the Thimble Islands. After that he lost sight of them.

When the motorboat disappeared, Tony was off Sachem Head. He wanted to continue but remembered his promise to Grandma that he would stay close to home.

After a moment's indecision, Tony told himself that since he already had gone back to the harbor, this was his *second* time out. He hadn't made any promise about *that*. Gripping the tiller tightly, he aimed for the Thimble Islands.

After reaching Clark's Point, Tony sailed toward Harrison Point. From there he traveled south in the direction of the islands. It wasn't long before he reached the first of them, the one called Narrows Island.

Among the islands, Tony discovered that the wind shifted constantly. First it came from one direction, then another. More than once, while Tony was trying to figure the wind, the *Snark*'s dagger board smashed into a submerged rock. The jolt was as unnerving as it was unexpected. Tony couldn't imagine how any bigger ships could get through. They would sink. Fast.

As Tony sailed the *Snark* on, twisting and turning among the islands, it was hard to see very far. Tony had the feeling he was in a maze. Sometimes he'd cut around and find himself in the sound. Then he'd head back in among the islands, only to come out on another side, but *which* side he didn't know.

Still, Tony was happy just to be sailing. He loved the way he could move in, around, between the many islands. He forgot about the people in the motorboat. He didn't pay particular attention to where he was or where he was heading. Only the occasional submerged rocks caused him concern.

It took a while before Tony realized he had lost track of how long he had been out. All he knew was that he was starting to feel hungry. It was time to go back home.

Cutting around a couple of the islands, Tony kept thinking he'd get a clear view of Swallows Bay Harbor. He did not.

Puzzled, he moved farther in the direction he had been going, only to see a whole new group of islands. He reversed himself. Now it was as if he had entered into a new maze. Gradually he began to grasp what had happened.

He was lost.

CHAPTER 9

Tony felt more stupid than nervous. The notion of being lost in a boat seemed impossible. He attempted tacking randomly, trying to thread his way to a place he could recognize. But no matter where he sailed among the islands, he could not find his way. As more time passed—still without a familiar sighting—his nervousness increased. Then, as he rounded one of the smaller islands, he saw an anchored boat. A man was in it.

Thinking he might ask for directions, he aimed for it. But as he sailed closer he realized it was the motorboat he had been watching in Swallows Bay Harbor, the one with the treasure seekers. Painted white and yellow, she had sleek, powerful lines. A white flag with a red slash across it dangled from her stern. Tony had no idea what it meant.

As Tony sailed closer, something shot out of the water by the side of the motorboat. With its black color and oddly shaped face, Tony first thought it was a seal. Then he realized it was the woman. She was wearing a face mask. Scuba tanks were on her back.

Wanting to get closer so he could shout for directions, Tony sailed toward the boat. As he approached, the man noticed him.

"Hey!" the man called. "Keep away. Can't you see the flag?" He pointed to the one at the end of his boat. "Diving!"

Tony yelled back, "Can you tell me how to get back to Swallows Bay Harbor?"

"Keep away!" the man shouted.

Thinking he had not been heard, Tony continued to sail forward. "I'm trying to get to Swallows Bay Harbor," he called again.

"Keep clear!" the man cried, shaking a fist at him. "Away!"

Wondering what *that* was all about, feeling frustrated and disappointed, Tony came about. Once more he returned to the confusion of the islands, all his thoughts concentrated on getting home.

It took another half hour of tacking around among the islands before Tony emerged on the other side of Wayland Island. Once there, he was sure he was seeing Swallows Bay Harbor a mile and a half away. Feeling a sense of relief, Tony took direct aim at it.

Getting back—with the wind behind him—was not hard. The *Snark* moved quickly. Relaxed, certain he at last knew where he was and where he was going, Tony's thoughts went back to his meeting with the people in the motorboat.

It angered and puzzled him that the man had been so unfriendly. He saw no reason for it. Only gradually did a new thought come: The people on the motorboat were not *digging* for treasure, they were *diving* for it.

Grandma was waiting on the dock. Tony saw right away she was not happy.

"Am I late?"

"Tony, it's two-thirty," she said as he brought the boat to shore.

"I went over to the Thimble Islands," Tony explained, "and got lost. I didn't mean to."

"Tony," she said sternly, "if you are to sail around the world, you and I, we're going to have to work out an understanding."

"Maybe I could get a compass."

"Fine," Grandma snapped, making Tony realize how worried she'd been. "I will get you one. And a watch, too," she added. "You must be hungry."

"Sure am!"

"After you eat, we'll go get them."

As they went up to the house, Tony told her about seeing the treasure hunters. "You know what? They weren't digging. They were diving."

"In the islands?"

"Right. They even chased me off. I mean, they

didn't want me near. I was only asking for directions."

"Which island were they at?" Her tone had softened.

"Don't know."

"Look at the map. Maybe you'll figure it out."

Before eating, Tony got down the big map from the living room wall. It had been there for as long as Tony could remember. Now, for the first time, he really looked at it.

Most of the map was of the sound, just empty sea with bottom depths given. Tony studied the depth figures. In some places it was very deep, even though close to shore. There, too, was Swallows Bay Harbor, along with the nearby coast. As for the Thimble Islands, they were all there and all curiously named.

"Can you tell where you were?" Grandma asked.

Tony shook his head. "I was really mixed up. I didn't even know what direction I was going in."

"Compass," Grandma said, as if to remind herself.

"What kind of treasure would be under the water?" Tony asked.

"Wet," Grandma said with a smile.

"Look how deep it is here," Tony said. "But then, right next to it . . ."

Grandma shook her head. "Tony, that map is old. Ten years. Things shift."

"You should get a new map."

"Never mind maps. Just promise to stay close to shore. Then you can use your *olhos*."

"*Olhos?*"

"Eyes."

Once Tony had eaten, they left for Guilford in search of a compass and watch. As they were walking down Main Street to the sporting goods store, they passed an antique shop.

"Look!" Tony called. In the window of the antique store was a ship model very much like the one that was sitting on his dresser. "How come it's there?" he asked.

"*Caro.*"

"*Caro?*"

"Expensive. And old."

"Do you think mine is as old?"

"I told you, your grandfather, he got it at a junk sale."

"It could still be old."

"Maybe . . ."

"Grandma, ours is called the *Swallow*. If it *is* old, maybe it has something to do with the naming of the harbor. . . ."

"Tony, you may be Portuguese and the Portuguese are always fine sailors. That doesn't keep them from drowning or getting lost, or being late for lunch and making their grandmas worried. You need the compass and watch. Come on now. The treasure can wait."

CHAPTER 10

As they drove back, Tony said, "Want to come out in the boat with me?"

Grandma paled. *"Me?"*

"Sure. Maybe you'd feel better if you saw how well I did."

After a moment of quiet, Grandma said, "Tony, I must make a confession. I am not comfortable in boats."

Tony laughed. "I thought you said all Portuguese were good sailors."

"Nothing is *all*."

"You can try, can't you?"

"I suppose. . . ."

Back home, Tony changed. "Aren't you going to wear a bathing suit?" he asked his grandma.

A sheepish look filled her broad face. "I do not have one," she answered.

"You're kidding."

"Tony, I never learned to swim. So you must make certain we don't fall over."

Grandma—wearing a life jacket borrowed from the Carlucis—took a seat up front in the *Snark*. "Do you have your compass? Your watch?" she asked, clutching nervously to the sides.

Tony showed her that he'd tied the compass around his neck with a piece of string and held up his wrist to show her the watch was there. "Any more excuses?" he asked.

"I think not," Grandma grunted.

Tony pushed the boat out and jumped in. Right away he caught a breeze. They began to move through the harbor. Grandma did not look very comfortable.

"Tony," she cautioned, "not too far."

"Some pirate you'd make," Tony teased.

"You can tease. But if you make me wet, I will make you walk a plank!"

Tony, laughing, took them to Joshua Cove. "It's very shallow here," he told her.

"*Bom.*"

Back and forth they sailed, Tony not doing much of anything except showing off his new skills.

"You do very well," Grandma told him. "I am much reassured. Thank you."

Pleased with himself, Tony headed back for the harbor. As they sailed in, they were passed by a motorboat.

"Grandma," Tony whispered, "that's them! The ones I saw diving in the Thimbles."

Grandma turned to look.

Tony sailed as close as he could to the now-moored motorboat.

As they went by, the woman in the boat looked up. Tony turned away quickly, hoping he'd been fast enough. But as he continued on, he had the sensation that eyes were watching him.

"What do you think?" Tony asked.

"They did not look at you pleasantly."

Tony allowed himself a quick glance at the motorboat. "They're staring at us," he said.

"Tony, *please!* Don't make them mad at you."

"I'm just looking."

"I am serious," Grandma warned.

"Don't worry."

When the *Snark* drew close to the shore, Grandma said, "Now, just because I'm going home, you don't have to. You can go out again."

"Really?"

"But—Tony, look at me, not at that boat—you must not get lost. Or bother those people. Or sink or be back later than six o'clock. Can you do all that?"

Tony grinned. "Sure."

"What time is it?"

Tony checked his watch. " 'Bout five."

"Be home in one hour. Do we agree?"

"Aye, aye, sir," he called as he pushed off.

Tony thought he would just sail around outside of the harbor. But as he started off, he noticed that the people in the motorboat were climbing into a dingy. They were heading for the dock.

Hoping he wasn't being obvious, Tony tacked across the harbor. He stayed as far away from the motorboat as possible, but he always kept the couple in view. He saw them reach the dock, walk to shore, get into a car, and drive off. As soon as Tony saw their car disappear, he swung back toward their boat.

Tony had no intention of getting into their boat. All he wanted was a better look inside. So when he came along it he stood up—hand to the *Snark*'s mast—and peered in. The digging equipment was lying right there. In a glance it was obvious that the tools had *never* been used. In that instant Tony felt certain that the tools were there only to make people *think* they were digging.

Tony jibed away, ready to go out of the bay. As he turned, he glanced back toward the shore. There was the car Tony thought had gone. Not only had the couple come back, they were standing beside their car. The man was holding a pair of binoculars up to his eyes. Tony was sure they had seen everything he had done.

Trying to act as if he hadn't noticed them, Tony sailed out of the harbor as smoothly as he could. But once out, he was satisfied he had gotten out of a potentially unpleasant moment. Now he lay back and stretched his legs forward. One hand was on the tiller. His head rested atop the stern. From that position he could keep his eyes forward even as he listened to the soft slap of the water at the bow, the flutter of the sail.

As usual the warm wind was coming out of the south. The easy tension of the rudder in his hand was a pleasure. In a dreamy mood—there was nothing above but blue sky and high clouds—Tony sailed slowly across Sachem Head. Clark's Point lay before him.

Suddenly, Tony heard the whine of a motor. At first he didn't make much of it. He kept his eyes forward. But when the noise persisted, even grew louder, he sat up and looked to see where it was coming from. It was the motorboat, the one he had been watching. The couple was following him.

Hoping it was just a coincidence, Tony decided to act as if their coming didn't matter. Even so, he tried to gradually turn the *Snark* about. When the couple moved with him, forcing him back, Tony began to feel small and alone.

Wanting to be nearer land, he steered the *Snark* so that he was now heading into the bay between Sachem Head and Clark's Point. The motorboat continued to follow.

More and more nervous, Tony decided just being close to shore was not enough. He wanted to be on land. And he wanted to get there quickly. He came about hard, heading toward Clark's Point itself.

The couple in the motorboat reacted just as fast. Tony heard them kick up the motor. He glanced back—and swallowed hard. The motorboat was heading right toward him. Tony attempted to maneuver closer to shore. While the motorboat gained rapidly, the *Snark* reacted sluggishly. Then, just as the *Snark*'s dagger board scraped bottom, the motorboat bore down within four feet then peeled sharply off, sending out a wash of waves strong enough to capsize the *Snark*.

Tony, flung overboard, plunged underwater but quickly shot to the surface. In the shallow water, his legs touched bottom. Twisting around, he searched for the motorboat. It was not far off. The couple were looking at him, watching to see what he would do. Not that they said anything. They didn't have to. Tony grasped the message: "Stop bothering us!"

As the couple headed out toward the sound, Tony dealt with the *Snark*. He worked the way Chris had shown him, pushing the dagger board down, pivoting the boat up, then bailing.

When the sailboat was finally empty of water, Tony swung himself in and set his course for home. He had no doubts that those people were trying to frighten him. In part they had succeeded. But they had also made him more determined than ever to find out what it was they wanted so much to hide.

CHAPTER 11

During dinner, Tony told Grandma what had happened. She was angry and upset.

"You have to be careful," she warned. "They could have gotten you drowned."

"They weren't trying to *drown* me," Tony insisted. "Only force me into shallow water. And they watched. They were just warning me to keep away."

"I think you should tell Chris's brother—the harbor master."

That night, Tony laid out the map of the Thimble Islands on the dining room table. He had already studied it for more than an hour when Grandma came to look over his shoulder.

"Did you find anything interesting?" she asked.

"Chris says the names of places around here mean things."

"So?"

Tony pointed to one of the islands. "Money Island," he said.

"And what do you think Money Island means?"

"The treasure."

"Tony, I am uncomfortable with you looking out there with those people about."

"Don't worry."

"But I do worry!"

After giving up on the map, Tony began to go through one of the library books he had borrowed. It was about old-time ships in Connecticut. A scholarly book, it was not easy reading. But it did have some interesting pictures and maps.

Tony was flipping through the book, ready to put it aside, when he noticed a section at the back of the book:

SHIPWRECKS OFF
THE CONNECTICUT COAST

There were entries like

1721. DUKE OF NORFOLK. *Captain Joseph Bozza. Out of Boston. Beached on Fisher's Island. All hands saved.*

and

1739. DOLPHIN. *Captain Brewster Kirmmse.*
Out of Copenhagen. Off Mystic during hurri-
cane. Salvaged.

Intrigued, Tony began to turn the pages, looking to
see what he might find. Suddenly he started.
"Grandma!"
"What's the matter?"
He ran to her with the book. "Look at this!"
"What am I looking at?"
"It's a list of shipwrecks in old-time Connecticut.
Look at that," Tony said, pointing to an entry.

1777. SWALLOW. *Captain Samuel Bab-*
bitt. British Navy payroll ship. Out of Bristol.
Lost in storm somewhere along coast between
New Haven and New London. No known
survivors.

"What," Grandma said, "am I to think of that?"
"That boat model upstairs is called the *Swallow*."
"So you say. . . ."
"And this *is* Swallows Bay Harbor."
"True . . ."
"And those guys are looking for treasure in the water
around here. Bet it's connected to this." Tony pointed
to the entry in the book.
"How?"

"Maybe the *Swallow*, the *real* one, sank nearby. It fits, sort of. Right? Between New Haven and New London. In the Thimbles. There are so many rocks there. Enough to sink ships."

"Okay."

"Don't you see, that's where those people were looking. 'No known survivors,' " Tony continued. "But maybe Littlejohn *was* a survivor. The *only* one. So he knows the wreck is out there somewhere, full of money—a payroll—and he comes *here* to look. Bet he didn't tell anyone where he came from because he was British. You know, the Revolution and all. Anyway, he wants that treasure for himself. Get it?"

"Possible."

"But he didn't find it. That's why he's still looking."

"*Still?* What do you mean?"

"The statue. He's looking out toward the islands. Can we go into Guilford tomorrow morning?"

"For what?"

"I want to ask about Grandpa's ship model in that antique place."

The antique store opened at eleven. Tony and Grandma were waiting on the doorstep, model in hand, when the owner appeared.

"Good morning. Good morning," he said as he unlocked the door. "Come right on in. Let me get the lights a-shining." He was an old, white-haired man, cane in hand, but he bustled with lots of energy.

The shop was cluttered with everything from a walrus tusk to an old-fashioned typewriter.

Once the lights were on, the old man came forward. "Now, then, what can I do for you folks?"

"My name is Mrs. Souza," Grandma informed him. "This is my grandson Tony. We're from Swallows Bay."

"Pleasure . . ."

"Tony, he saw that ship model in your window. And he thought it looked like the one he has here. What he would like is for you to look at it."

"Sure thing. Bring it on over here, son."

Tony carried the model to a table and set it down. The dealer, making soft clucking noises, studied it carefully.

"Well now, Tony—that your name?—you've got sharp eyes."

"Is it old?" Tony asked.

"You bet. Nineteenth century," said the dealer. "Fact, I should say it's older than the one I've got in my window. That one's about 1850. I'd figure this one was, say, about 1810. She got a name anywhere?"

Tony said, "It's called the *Swallow*."

"That so?"

"On the sterncastle."

The man squinted at the letters. "You could be right," he said. He turned to Grandma. "You folks interested in selling it? It might be worth something."

"It belongs to Tony," Grandma replied.

"What do you say, young fellow?"

"How much?"

"I don't know. Maybe two . . . four hundred. Or more."

"That much?"

"Oh, sure. If it's truly old. I'd have to do some more checking."

"Can you tell anything more about it?"

"Let's see now. It's a model of a frigate, popular design in the late eighteenth and early nineteenth centuries. Standard British Navy ship, which saw lots of action during the American Revolution and Napoleonic Wars.

"I will say," he continued, "it doesn't look to have been made by a professional model maker. I'd give a guess and say yours was an amateur job. Perhaps a sailor who was on the real ship."

"The *Swallow*?" Tony asked.

"Could be. Kind of a memory, if you see my meaning."

Tony shot a knowing look at Grandma.

"Not an uncommon practice," the dealer went on. "Where did you get it?"

"My husband, he found it in a yard sale."

"Good for him."

"Anything else?" Tony asked.

"Let's think. . . . There was a tradition that model makers put their own names inside the boat."

"*Inside?*"

"The captain's cabin. As if they were sailing her. A nice touch, don't you think?"

"Does this one have that?" Tony wondered.

"Let's have a look-see." The dealer took the boat under the strong light of a lamp and tried to peer into the tiny cabin beneath the sterncastle.

"Sorry," the man said.

"What's the matter?" Tony asked.

"Portholes blocked. Can't see a thing. And I'm afraid the only way I'd be able to see would be to pry this here part off." He tapped the top of the sterncastle. "I shouldn't like to do that. Might hurt her. And she not being mine . . ."

He handed the boat back to Tony. "Lovely old thing, though. Lovely. Makes me wonder where she comes from. You let me know if you want to make some money from her, son. Always glad to talk."

CHAPTER 12

"There really is a treasure," Tony insisted as they drove back. "No, listen. This is a model of that British ship that sank. The *Swallow*. Bet you anything the real one sank in the Thimble Islands. Probably full of payroll money, too."

"Tony . . ."

"Grandma, I *know* it. I mean, that book practically *said* so. Except somebody *did* survive. Littlejohn. Only he wasn't the captain. I think he just said he was, and spent all his time looking for that treasure."

"Maybe yes, maybe no," Grandma said with a frown of worry. "Doesn't mean money is still there."

"You can't tell if you don't look," Tony reminded her. "Bet you anything that's what those people are doing."

"You told me that Steve said people don't get to keep sea treasure."

"Right. That's the whole point. Those people are trying to *steal* it."

Grandma glanced at her grandson. "I think you watch too much TV."

"Grandma, it's true!"

"Okay," Grandma said after a moment. "But my mind is changed. I don't think you should look for the treasure."

"Why?" Tony said, taken by surprise.

"It's those people. Did you tell Chris's brother about them?"

"You don't have to worry!"

"Tony, first you say they are thieves. Then you say, nothing to worry about. It makes me uneasy." Grandma shook her head. "That man in the store, he said he'd give you lots of money for the model. Tony, you want money; you can do that."

"I know. But . . ."

"But what?"

Tony stroked the side of the model. "This is nice . . . but I keep thinking what could be out *there*."

"I don't want you to," Grandma said.

Once home, Grandma phoned Chris and asked her if she could come over after lunch.

"Did something happen with Tony yesterday?" Chris asked.

"Well, yes and no. I just think we need advice."

"I'll be there."

Chris came at about twelve-thirty, just in time for dessert.

"Tony," Grandma said, "start by telling Chris that, you know, the business."

Tony told Chris what happened in the islands, and how after, the people in the motorboat swamped him.

Chris was mad. "They can get a heavy fine for doing that," she said. "Did you get their boat registration number?"

Tony shook his head.

"If you see them again," Chris suggested, "get it. It's on the bow. Give it to Steve. He'll talk to them. Wonder if they'll come back. I haven't seen them around."

"Now," Grandma said, "tell her the rest."

Tony explained everything he had found out about the treasure, as well as his guesses about it.

When he was done, Chris said nothing.

"Don't you think that the treasure could be real?" he pressed.

"I don't know . . ." Chris said cautiously. "Like I told you. People—not from here—do search around. Except, I never heard of anyone finding anything. Actually, we sort of joke about it."

"What I think," Grandma said sternly, "is that we should forget all about it. Don't you?" she asked Chris.

"To tell you the truth, Mrs. Souza," Chris said, "what I'm thinking mostly about is those people dunking Tony. That's not right. Could be dangerous. As for the rest . . . Look, if there were a treasure, I'd have to think someone would have found it by now."

"The bottom could have shifted," Tony pointed out.

"Sure, but . . ."

"Would you at least help me look?" Tony begged.

Grandma leaned forward and touched Tony's arm. "Tony, listen to Chris. I think I made a mistake to say you should look. I'm pretty sorry about that. I just don't feel good thinking of you out there with those people."

"But—"

Chris cut in. "Hey, sailor, we going out for a lesson today?"

"I guess," Tony said, feeling discouraged.

Tony and Chris met at three o'clock by the dock. With Tony at the tiller from the start, they sailed into the sound. It was deeper and rougher there. Chris thought it good practice.

The only talk was about sailing. But as they approached the harbor on the way home, Tony said, "Don't you think you could help me look for that treasure a little bit?"

"I'd like to, Tony," said Chris. "Really, I would. But it would take a lot of time, and I don't have any. I'm supposed to be at the store. It's a regular job. And I've got tons of other stuff to do. Tell you what, though.

If you need me for anything special, you can always let me know."

Tony studied her. "You don't think there is a treasure, do you?"

Chris shook her head ruefully. "Tony," she said, "I wish it *were* true."

Tony tried not to show his disappointment. "What about more lessons?"

"You've got the basics. The rest is practice and experience. Just don't get yourself out too far. With a little boat like this, it doesn't make much sense. Like I told you, respect the sea and the wind. And one other thing . . ."

"What's that?"

"If you do see that motorboat—and those people . . . Want to know what I really think?"

"I guess. . . ."

"Do yourself a favor. Keep away."

That night, Tony could not fall asleep. He kept thinking about ships and sailing and the treasure. Finally he got out of bed and picked up the model of the *Swallow*, turning it all about. He glanced at the clock beside his bed. It was eleven-thirty. Grandma would be asleep.

Carrying the ship model carefully with both hands, Tony made his way down to the kitchen. There he fetched a little knife that his grandma used for peeling fruit. Using its point he gently ran the knife around the entire top part of the sterncastle. Old glue fell away in dark curls. Working even more slowly, Tony forced the blade around the top deck's edge, prying it up.

It lifted a fraction of an inch. Encouraged, Tony worked more, trying to keep from going too fast. He did not want to break or crack anything.

Bit by bit, the top eased off. Tony could feel his heart thumping. Now the tiny cabin inside the sterncastle was exposed.

On the inside—on the floor of the miniature cabin—was what looked like a ring, a ring enclosing a piece of glass. Tony reached in and touched it. The ring broke away. He picked it up. At first he couldn't tell what it was. He looked through the glass. Everything was very big. It was a lens.

He looked back into the boat model. The lens had been held in place by a blob of something yellow. Tony flicked it with a finger. The blob broke away. He picked it up. It felt waxy. When he sniffed at it, it smelled like wax, too.

Once more he peered into the cabin. Now he realized that under the place where the wax had been were tiny letters, so small he couldn't read them.

More and more excited, Tony placed the ship below the lamp that dangled over the kitchen table. Then he brought his eyes close up to the tiny cabin and, using the small magnifying lens, looked at the letters.

What he read was

Ezra Littlejohn, Quartermaster

CHAPTER *13*

Tony was sitting in the kitchen when Grandma came down.

"You're the early one," she said.

"Restless," he admitted.

She looked out of a window. "Doesn't look very good today," she said. "The weatherman, he said there was a good chance of rain. That means fog, too."

"I'm still going out," Tony announced.

"Oh? Where?"

"Just sailing around," Tony said evasively. In his pocket he fingered the little lens.

"When will you be back?"

"Can I take my lunch?" Tony countered.

"You going treasure hunting?"

"Not really."

Grandma Souza looked at him carefully. "Is that a yes or no?"

"No," Tony finally said.

77

Grandma remained still for such a long time that Tony said, "*Can* I go sailing?"

"Tony, listen to me. Tomorrow I have to go to a doctor's appointment in New Haven. I don't want you to go out unless you sail with Chris."

"Grandma, Chris said it was *okay* for me to sail alone."

"I know she did. But I still worry. Because of what those people did to you."

"What about today?" Tony asked.

Grandma took another look out the window. "Today, yes, but I want you to come back by noon."

"One o'clock," Tony countered.

"Okay."

"I'll take my watch," Tony said.

"And compass," Grandma reminded him. "But Tony, you must promise me that if the weather turns bad, no matter what time, you'll come right back."

"Okay."

She looked him right in the eyes. "We agree then. You said today—but with *no* treasure hunting—and home by one. Then, no sailing tomorrow. Maybe you'll come with me when I go to the doctor. We'll do something special. Okay?"

"Okay."

As Tony walked to the water, he stopped and studied the Captain Littlejohn statue. Once more he gazed at the spyglass in the captain's hand, then turned to look out over the water. Hadn't Ezra Littlejohn designed his own statue? Maybe it meant he *wanted* to be staring right where he had spent his life looking for the treasure.

Suddenly he had an idea. Rushing back home, Tony got a small screwdriver, then returned to the statue. Standing on the statue's pedestal, he began to poke at the tube. Bit by bit the accumulated dirt inside fell away. Tony's first discovery was that a lens was still in the front end.

Tony pressed his eye to the small end of the spyglass, looking to see where it was aimed. It seemed to be aimed at the Thimble Islands, all right, but things looked tiny, too tiny to see anything.

Frustrated, Tony started to climb down, only to stop. *The lens*. Back up he went. With fumbling fingers he took the other lens—the one he had found in the *Swallow* model—from his pocket and placed it in the big end of the spyglass. The lens was too small. But when he tried that lens in the small end, it fit perfectly.

Once more Tony swung about and pressed an eye to the spyglass. Everything was now large and clear. He was seeing three islands. Which three?

After peering through the spyglass again, Tony stood up and gazed across the water, trying to fix in his mind which islands they were. Then, scooping out the lens, he jumped down, ran back home, and studied the wall map.

The more he looked at the map, the more sure he was that he had been looking at three islands: East Stooping Bush. Hoghead. And Money. Tony felt his heart leap. *Money!*

Thirty minutes later, Tony was sailing the *Snark* out of Swallows Bay Harbor. He had his compass around his neck. His watch was on his wrist. A plastic bag of fruit, as well as a jar of water, were in the bow.

As he left the harbor, he checked to see if the motorboat had returned. It had not. Perhaps, he thought, those people had gotten scared about what they had done to him and decided not to bother anymore. That would be just fine with him. Tony set the *Snark*'s course toward Joshua Cove and Sachem Head, slow but easy.

Though the day was gray, the sound was calm. The swell was only slightly higher than normal. The wind, as usual, was coming out of the south. Tony felt good and in full command.

It was only when he came near Sachem Head that the telltale atop the mast let him know that the wind had begun to shift. It was now coming from the west. Tony had no idea what that meant, if anything. All he did was adjust the way he was sailing, pleased he knew how.

Off Sachem Head, he brought the *Snark* sharply about. Soon he had reached Harrison Point. Once there he had to make up his mind in which direction to go.

He intended to keep his word not to go treasure hunting. But nothing had been said about seeing if he could find the place where he had seen the people diving. That, he felt, was fair. He was prepared to bet anything it would be close to the islands—his hopes were on Money Island—that he had seen through Littlejohn's spyglass.

Tony glanced at the sky. The weather was only a little worse. A bit darker.

With a firm turn of the rudder, Tony aimed the *Snark* south. Soon he was off Narrows Island. He had reached the Thimbles.

But when Tony attempted to sail toward Money Island, he could not. To go that way meant heading into the wind. He had to tack toward Flying Point, then swing back around toward Cut-in-Two and Dogfish islands. Only then was he able to come back down toward Money. The wind had shifted that much.

Still, it wasn't much later that Tony was coming down past Davis Island, just as lost as he had been the day before. This time, however, there was a difference. He had a compass. And he had studied the map. If he didn't know exactly where he was, at least— or so he told himself—he had a much better sense of his position. He sailed on, feeling almost lazy.

It was while coming down the west coast of Money

Island, on the way to Puddle Island, that he suddenly saw the couple and their boat.

By the southern tip of Money Island lay a much smaller island, Hoghead. It was right in the channel *between* Money and Hoghead that Tony, looking east, saw them anchored.

Elated by his discovery, certain they had not seen him, Tony continued sailing south until he was off Puddle Island. There he threw the *Snark*'s bow into the wind, allowing himself a pause to think out what to do.

He knew what he *wanted* to do: spy on the couple and find out exactly what they were doing. He saw no harm in *that*. He understood it had to be done carefully, without his being seen. But that, he decided, was not going to be very hard.

The best way to do it, the safest way would be for him to sail west, go around High Island, turn north, then go completely around West Crib Island, then continue east. Finally, he would be able to come back south.

He would have made a big circle. But it would enable him to reach Hoghead Island on the side *opposite* from where the couple was anchored.

Tony set off.

CHAPTER 14

Tony's plan turned out to be difficult to execute. First the wind shifted, until it was coming out of the north. It blew harder, too, tossing the sea. The choppy water, flecked with whitecaps, reminded Tony of sugar frosting.

But determined to watch the couple, Tony continued on. Even so, it was a while before he had the wind at his back. Then down he flew, between Money and East Stooping Bush. So quickly did he shoot past the channel off Money and Hoghead—the place where he had hoped to view the couple's motorboat—that he saw nothing—except that they were still there. That made him realize that spying from the *Snark* was not going to work. Besides, if he kept sailing up and down that way, they would more than likely see him. No, it was clear to Tony that if he really wanted to see what they were doing, he would have to do it from a position on land. With hardly a further thought, Tony came about and headed north for Hoghead.

Hoghead Island, though small, was covered with bushes and trees. That suited Tony fine. It would provide lots of cover for hiding. But the island was also ringed with rocks. That made it difficult for the *Snark* to approach. In fact, at first Tony didn't think he could even get to the island. It took a number of tries to discover a channel wide enough to enable him to sail the *Snark* close to a strip of sandy shore. There he hopped into the knee-deep water and pulled the sailboat in the last few feet. From there he stepped ashore.

Worried that he had already taken too much time, Tony hurriedly wedged the prow of the *Snark* between two rocks. He did consider tying the boat up, but there was nothing at hand. Then, even as he was trying to make up his mind about that, he realized it was past noon, close to the time he had promised to be home. Should he spy on the couple or turn back?

Tony told himself that, after all, he *was* there. And what he was going to do would not take long, plus he would hurry.

Just before leaving the *Snark*, Tony realized that the bright orange color of his life jacket could be too easily noticed. Hastily, he stripped it off and flung it into the boat.

Scrambling over the rocks that ringed the little

beach, Tony got among the trees. But the island—which appeared to be nothing but a big pile of rocks jumbled together—proved difficult to get through. Trees were extremely thick. Prickly brambles were everywhere. Underfoot there was hardly any smooth place for normal walking at all.

Though it took longer than he thought it would, Tony managed to get to the other side of the island. From behind a tree, he was able to look out over the channel. There they were. He had aimed perfectly.

Tony guessed that the channel between Hoghead Island, where he was, and Money Island, across the way, was no more than fifty yards. He had no way of knowing how deep it was. It could have been forty feet deep. It could have been four. As for the motorboat, it was anchored right in the middle.

The man was in sight. He was sitting in the motorboat wearing a black wet suit and looking down into the water. The woman, Tony decided, must be underwater.

Sure enough, as Tony watched, the woman broke surface a few feet away from the boat. She had a face mask on. A tank of oxygen was on her back.

As soon as she came up, she spat her mouthpiece out and shouted, "Got another!" She held up a hand which clutched something. Tony couldn't see what it was.

The man took what she offered and studied it carefully. Then the two talked, but Tony was unable to make out their words.

Finally, the man in the boat stood up. Tony saw him look up at the sky. It was getting darker. That didn't seem to bother the man. He got on his own diving equipment.

The woman, meanwhile, dove back down. It wasn't long before the man slipped into the water, quickly disappearing beneath the surface.

With both people underwater, Tony didn't feel so cautious. He came out from behind the tree and boldly examined the channel. To his disappointment, there wasn't much to see.

It was then that Tony remembered Chris's suggestion, that, if possible, he should get the motorboat's registration number. He knew it was on the prow of the boat. But because of the way the boat was anchored in the channel, he couldn't quite read it. But if he shifted his position just a little, he would be able to see it quite clearly.

With the woman and man still underwater, Tony saw his opportunity. At the last moment he checked himself. How long, he wondered, would they *stay* under water? He recollected that they did have air tanks on their backs. That must mean they could stay down a long while, more than the time he'd need to check the boat's number. Tony decided to take the chance.

As quickly as he could, he started to walk across

atop the waterfront rocks so as to see the motorboat's prow. Walking was not easy. Concentrating hard, he had to extend his arms wide to keep a balance as he edged across.

When he got as far as he could, he turned and looked across the channel. When he did he found himself staring right into the face of one of the divers.

CHAPTER 15

It was the man.

Both he and Tony were so startled that they gazed at each other dumbly for a long moment. It was the man who reacted first. Spitting out his mouthpiece, he yelled, "Hey!"

Tony jumped off the rocks and raced for the trees. Hearing splashing behind, he was sure the couple was coming after him. Into the closeknit trees he plunged, jumping from rock to rock, sometimes slipping but always scrambling up. On he went. When there weren't rocks, there were trees and bushes to push through. But after a few minutes of fighting his way, he realized he was not even sure he was heading in the right direction.

Panting for breath, he made himself stop. Where was he? Should he go this way or that?

From behind, he heard the boat motor come to life.

Now he was certain the couple was trying to get around to the other side where he was heading—before he could—to cut him off. He had to get to the *Snark*.

Dashing from rock to rock, Tony slipped, twisting his ankle. Despite the momentary pain, he refused to hold back, but kept crashing on until—it seemed to take forever—he burst out on the water's edge. The *Snark* was nowhere in sight.

Tony's first thought was that he had come to the wrong place. He jumped back among the trees, only to halt when he realized he had no idea which way to go.

Bewildered, his fearfulness increasing every second, he returned to the place where he had first looked for the boat. Maybe they had taken it. He checked again, searching about for some clue. This time he saw his own footprints where he had first come up on the shore. It made him certain he had returned to the same spot where he had wedged the *Snark*. He glanced out over the sound. And saw her. She was drifting away.

Tony jumped into the water and began to wade after the *Snark*. But when the water reached his chest, he had to stop. The sailboat was too far out, and it was moving even farther away.

As Tony stood in the chilly water, he realized what must have happened. During the time he had been on the other side of the island, the tide had come in just enough to lift the *Snark* off the rocks where he had carelessly wedged her. Now she was adrift.

Even as he stood in the water watching the *Snark* drift off, Tony heard the throb of the motorboat from the far side of the island. The couple was *not* coming after him; they were heading away. Now Tony's one thought was that he must reach them, call them, get them to take him off.

Back to the other side he tore. But when he reached the channel where he had watched them before, all that remained was the faint, diminishing sound of their motor. They were gone, and he was alone on the island.

It was a dismal Tony who stood gazing out over the empty water. Even as he stood there, a thin rain began to fall. It began to get colder, too. Goose bumps rose on his arms.

Fighting back tears, Tony retreated among the trees. There he attempted to calm himself. As his panic eased, he was convinced there was only one thing to do: He had to find a way to get back to the mainland.

The first thing—the only thing—that came to mind was the notion of swimming from island to island. It would be a way to gradually work his way back. As he recalled from his grandma's map, the mainland wasn't that far. Once there, he could walk home. Or call. Grandma would be able to come and get him.

But Tony also remembered that there were some rather large gaps between a few of the islands. Hadn't Chris said some places were really deep? Which ones he could not remember. Though he had always thought of himself as a good swimmer, confronted with this kind of swim he began to doubt his ability.

Unable to think what else to do, he made up his mind that he'd at least try to swim toward the mainland. To further reassure himself, he vowed that he would decide about going farther at each island.

Tony returned to the water's edge. Trying to ignore the rain, he eyed the channel between Hoghead Island and Money Island. He was sure he had swum as far in races at the Y. Or had he?

He sat on a rock and took off his sneakers, using their laces to tie them to the belt loops on his trousers.

Nervously, he waded into the water. Maybe he could walk across. The rocks on the bottom felt sharp. He shivered.

Six more steps brought him into deep water. Any hope that the channel might be shallow—like Joshua Cove—evaporated. If he wanted to get off the island, wading would not do. Swimming was necessary. He wished he had kept his life jacket.

Tony studied the channel again. The shore of Money Island was dim. The rain had become a thick fog, making it even harder for him to see. He checked his compass, dangling from the ribbon tied around his neck. He would be swimming northeast. He looked at his watch. It was almost one.

Tony waded farther into the channel. Cold water swirled around his chest. His heart pounded. He kept telling himself that Money Island wasn't *that* far, that he had swum that distance plenty of times, that it would only get harder if he waited, that there was no other way to get home.

After taking one more deep breath, Tony dove in.

CHAPTER 16

Though Tony was a good swimmer, most of his swimming had been done in pools, or at protected beaches. The channel was very different. No sooner did he hit the water, kicking his legs, swinging his arms for all he was worth, than he felt himself being swept hard to one side by a powerful current. It was not the direction he wanted to go.

His first reaction was to fight back. When that didn't help, when the powerful drift continued, he tried to stop himself by lowering his feet. Too late. It was too deep.

Shaking his head clear, struggling to keep cool, Tony attempted to tread water. For a moment he held place. With that came calmness. But the calmness began to fade when his energy lagged and he began to be pushed farther from Money Island.

Abruptly, Tony decided he must get back to Hoghead Island. It took only a few strokes in that direction to see how ineffective he was. The press of the water was too much. He could not go back.

Now Tony twisted around. Once again he began to take wild strokes in the direction—he thought—of Money Island. He managed to make some headway. Moving in the right direction even eased his feeling of helplessness. He settled down and began to swim with steadier strokes.

Five minutes later he was forced to rest. Treading water, he made another attempt to see where he was. The shore he had been aiming for no longer looked like Money Island. Had he turned himself around *back* toward Hoghead? Was he going somewhere else? His struggle, and the fog, had confused him.

Trying to resist a renewed onset of panic, Tony let his feet down, hoping that there was a bottom he could touch. There was not. There was nothing else to do but gulp down more air and move his arms steadily to keep afloat.

Tony now realized it didn't matter where he was. Reaching land, *any* land, was what he had to do. He began to swim again. This time, he knew all too well, he was swimming for his life.

He made more progress than before. And as he continued to press on, he sensed he was no longer in the swiftly moving channel. Wherever he was, the tidal flow was greatly reduced. The fog grew thinner, too.

He could even make out a shore. A surge of self-assurance gave him new strength. It was no longer an impossible distance.

Bit by bit the shore he was heading for loomed larger. He knew he was going to make it. The more he knew it, the stronger he felt. Suddenly, one of his sneakers dropped off.

Once more he lowered his feet in hopes of touching bottom. It was still impossible. Should he leave the sneaker or not?

Looking at the land, he could make out rocks, lots of them. He was going to need that sneaker to walk. His renewed sense of confidence decided for him. He would dive for it.

Taking a swallow of air, hoping the bottom wasn't too deep, Tony flipped over, then dove below the water's surface. He kept his eyes open.

The water was about seven feet deep and murky. Fingers of seaweed waved gently. Plumes of sand, stirred by crabs, spurted up. The shadow of a fish flitted by. Along the bottom Tony could just make out alternate patches of rock and sand. White shells were scattered here and there. But no sneaker was in sight.

Tony bobbed back to the surface. Treading water, he told himself he was wasting his time and energy looking for the sneaker. He must get to shore. But the rocks . . . No, he needed that sneaker. He made up his mind to take no more than a couple more dives.

Trying to shift to a slightly different area, he plunged. At first he saw nothing. But, just as Tony came up, he thought he saw, out of the corner of his eye, a white patch. Was it the sneaker? He wasn't certain. He thought it was.

He shot up to the surface, took in some air, then—even while promising himself this would absolutely be his last try—he made another dive.

What he found below was a different kind of bottom than before, not nearly as flat. He was seeing small mounds, lots of them, covered with seaweed. There was also what looked like the crude outline of the bones of a gigantic fish. And, right in the midst of this—white against dark—Tony saw his sneaker.

Grabbing his sneaker, Tony kicked back to the surface. Once there, he panted for breath and clamped the sneaker between his teeth, then began to swim forcefully toward the shore.

It took a steady, rhythmic churn, but finally he was able to lower his toes to a firm bottom. In moments he was standing up. From there he walked—arms and legs trembling from exertion—the rest of the way to the shore.

Once on land he put on his sneakers. Uncomfortable and waterlogged as they were, he was grateful he had them. The stones were sharp underfoot. Wearily, he began to clamber over rocks until he found a small patch of sand. Paying no mind to the fog and drizzle, he flung himself down. Exhaustion flooded over him now. As though diving, he spread his arms wide. Wondering vaguely where he was, but glad beyond all else to be alive, he fell into a deep sleep.

CHAPTER 17

Tony opened his eyes to a sky of waning gray light. Whether it was the thick fog, the coming of a storm— perhaps he had slept longer than he meant to—whatever it was, the day was dimmer than when he had fallen asleep. And he was very hungry.

He looked at his watch. It had gone blank. It was ruined, he figured, by water. Ruefully, he realized they should have gotten a waterproof watch, not just one that was water resistant.

Then, when he reached for his compass, he discovered it was gone. He must have lost it swimming.

Gradually, Tony began to realize that not only didn't he know the time, he had not the slightest idea where he was. He did not even know in which direction was home.

Tony stood up and looked about. Though the island he was on appeared to be bigger than Hoghead, it was the same in other respects. A rocky shore surrounded an inland thick with clumps of stunted trees. The thought even occurred to him that perhaps it *was* Money Island.

Not knowing what else to do, but reminding himself of his plan to swim from island to island, Tony began to walk along the shore. As he walked, he kept his eyes to the water. His hope was that he'd get to see another nearby island.

But after a half hour of walking he had not seen another island, not one clue to suggest where he was. He kept telling himself it was because the fog was thick. There was nothing to do but keep walking.

He had reached a dead end, a dark, flat spit of sand broken by tufts of stiff eelgrass. Water lapped the shore on three sides. Then, for just a moment the fog lifted. Tony saw what appeared to be another island. What he could make of it—which wasn't much—suggested an island even smaller than Hoghead. But not only was it impossible to tell its size, it was hard for Tony to judge clearly how far away it was. Reluctantly, he decided it would be a mistake to swim for it unless he knew exactly where he was going. He realized he had been lucky before. As if Nature itself agreed, the misty island seemed to melt away, swallowed whole by the fog.

Tony looked around where he stood. The spit of land, he decided, was a lot like the place where he and Grandma had dug for clams. Just the thought of it reminded him of his hunger. He wished he had eaten his lunch. He had left it on the *Snark*.

On hands and knees he began to scoop out sand. Within moments he found five clams. After washing them at the water's edge, he cracked them one against the other, then pulled out the flesh, only to stop. Could he actually eat the stuff? *Raw?* He sniffed at one. Fishy. He stuck out his tongue and tasted of it. Not bad, he had to admit. As if to remind him of his hunger, his stomach growled. Tony nibbled the clam. It tasted good. He began to eat greedily.

Once having eaten, Tony felt much better, with energy considerably restored. He came off the spit and continued to explore the water's edge.

It was a wildly irregular shore along which he was moving, with countless inlets and small lagoons. Big boulders made it difficult to walk. And increasingly, Tony had the feeling that the lowering sky was closing down on him, locking him in.

It was getting damper, too. At first he thought it was just the fog becoming thicker. But it didn't take long for him to wonder if, in fact, night was coming on. Perhaps, after his hard swim across the channel, he had slept a lot longer than he'd thought.

Although he was getting nowhere, Tony preferred moving about to sitting and waiting for something to happen. Now and again he climbed a rock and turned complete circles on its top in search of anything that might help. He saw nothing.

Discouraged, Tony sat with his back against one of the big rocks. Save for the soft slap of waves upon the shore and the occasional cranky squawk of an invisible gull high above, it was eerily quiet. It was as if he were some kind of Robinson Crusoe on a faraway island. The thought gave him an odd feeling. He reminded himself that though it didn't *feel* like it, he was really quite close to the mainland and home.

The more he thought of it, the more the idea of spending a night on the island troubled Tony. That couple knew he was there. But maybe they just assumed he'd be able to get back on his own. After all, they apparently had nothing to do with the *Snark* floating away. He doubted then that they would tell anyone what had happened.

That meant Grandma wouldn't know anything. She must be terribly upset that he had not gotten back. She might be thinking he had drowned. Tony could almost sense her despair. Still, there wasn't much he could do except wait until the fog lifted. Once it did, he would at least be able to get a sense of his location. But that, he reminded himself, might not happen until the morning. If then. Feeling terrible about the mess he'd placed himself in, he got up and started to walk again.

There never seemed to be anything worth looking at. Between the growing dark and the fog, it all seemed hopeless. But it was while aimlessly rambling that he came upon the *Snark*.

He had not even been looking for her. All the same she was just *there*, her bow stuck precariously between some large boulders at the shore. Tony stood there, too surprised to do anything but stare at the sailboat. His first thought was that he was imagining her. But when he realized it *was* the *Snark*, his heart gave an extra beat. With as much joy as if he had found a long-lost friend, he rushed forward. He felt like hugging the boat.

How did it come back? All he could guess was that the complex currents that swirled about the islands, the ones that had tossed him about, had apparently brought her to that spot. And nothing, he knew, but blind luck had brought them back together.

Ravenously, he ate the fruit he'd left in the boat. And in a few short gulps he swallowed his remaining water.

Tony checked the boat carefully, trying to see if anything had been broken or lost. Everything appeared to be intact. Nothing gone or broken.

Certain the boat was in good shape, Tony did not have the smallest doubt in his mind about what he wanted to do: He would sail home.

Life jacket snugly on, he completed a hasty double

check to make sure everything was set. All he had to do was decide which direction to go in. That held him. He had no idea which direction was the right one. For all he knew he was facing the sound. Long Island Sound was twelve miles wide. And what—he suddenly asked himself—what if he inadvertently sailed toward the *ocean?* Or worse, into it?

Against that awful idea was the unpleasant thought of staying where he was, of spending the night there. He didn't want to do it, though he could almost hear his grandma—and Chris—insisting that was the thing to do. It was not long before his own cautious conscience joined the chorus of concern: *Don't sail.* Yet at the same time he was telling himself that since he had put himself into this mess, it was his responsibility to get out of it.

Frustrated, Tony stared out into the still, dark fog. More than anything he *wanted* to go, if only to show everybody he could handle himself. Anyway, he told himself, it wasn't really night yet. He should be able to get home before it got seriously dark, before Grandma got more worried than he guessed she was.

With a sudden impulsive move, Tony shoved the *Snark* out into the water, jumped in, grasped the sheet with one hand, and put his other hand to the tiller. For a moment the *Snark* seemed to be reluctant, even to tremble. Then, very slowly, Tony began to sail away from the island.

CHAPTER 18

As far as Tony was concerned, getting off the island was like being let out of jail. On all sides he had a feeling of unlimited space, of knowing he was entirely on his own. He took a deep breath and allowed himself to enjoy it.

Tony's sense of pleasure did not last long. Earlier in the day, when he had come to the Thimbles, there had been a strong wind. Now there was hardly a breeze. The sail flapped listlessly. The best the *Snark* could manage was a slow, quiet progress, almost an aimless drift. Now and again Tony trailed a finger into the water, then peered down to see if he was really moving. He was. But only barely.

Tony turned around to look back and see how far he had come. It was no longer possible to see the island he had left. In fact, there was nothing to see in any direction except the color gray. Gray water.

Gray sky. Gray fog. It was as if he were gliding into a deep and perhaps endless pocket.

It did not stay gray for long. It began to grow darker. And cooler.

Tony listened. The only sounds he heard were the faint gurgle of water against the hull, the slight creak of the *Snark* itself, his breathing. Tony kept telling himself that he wasn't far from land, that he was actually quite close. But the truth was he was becoming more and more upset.

It was not long before Tony admitted to himself that he had made a terrible mistake. He should never have gone off from the island. Not without a compass. He should have waited until the fog lifted, or for the night to pass, or for some light, or . . . anything but what he had done. What had Chris said? Respect the sea. It's always bigger than you. He had been very stupid.

Abruptly, he brought the *Snark* about, wanting nothing more than to get back to that island—whichever it was. At first he was satisfied he had made a U-turn. But after sailing awhile and not reaching the island— any island—he decided he had not aimed correctly. He turned another way. The result was equally useless. Once more he turned.

Tony tried to picture the map of Long Island Sound with its huge, white spaces of empty water, its spread of numbers showing water eighty, ninety feet deep.

He was afraid to keep going. He was just as afraid to turn again. The truth was he'd become afraid to do *anything*. Tears came to his eyes.

All the while the *Snark* kept gliding along as quietly, as gently as a leaf on a pond. Except Tony was acutely aware that he was not on a pond. For all he knew he was drifting directly toward the Atlantic Ocean.

Now and again a sudden puff of wind came up, causing the *Snark* to abruptly heel, bringing a sickening lurch to Tony's stomach. The boat would pick up speed. Then, just as suddenly, the wind died away. Calmness returned. The *Snark* floated on. Never had Tony felt so alone.

He lay down and stared straight up. The night grew darker. And cooler. In the cooler air, the fog evaporated. Stars began to appear: a few at first, but soon more and more until the entire dome of sky appeared to be salted with them.

Tony looked up in awe. Never before had he seen so many stars. They appeared to be very close, but at the same time immensely far away.

As the *Snark* glided on, Tony began to feel as if he were a part of these many stars, they a part of him. Perhaps, he thought, they were lost, too. Perhaps they were looking down at him and wondering where they were. The more he watched the stars, the more the sensation grew that all he had to do was reach out and he would be able to touch them where they lay, like him, adrift in the empty sea and sky. He was no longer alone. The thought proved a comfort.

Tony strained to listen for a sound. A foghorn. A boat. He heard nothing except the soft slap of the *Snark*'s bow as he continued to sail along.

How long he went on that way Tony did not know. It felt like hours. He was convinced he was moving out to sea, that there was no way for him to do anything to save himself, that he would drift forever. Perhaps when it grew light he would be able to come up with a plan.

To pass the time, he began to think about what had happened that day. His going to Hoghead. Watching the couple. Their seeing him. His race across the island and finding the *Snark* gone. His race back. His swim across the channel.

He stopped. Something caught his mind. He went over his swim again. He remembered what it was he had seen when diving for his sneaker, something like the bones of a great fish.

He wondered if it could have been the bones of a whale. They were big enough. True, he had never heard of whales in that part of the ocean. But then he reminded himself he really didn't know much about that kind of thing.

He tried to imagine what—considering the bones— a whale might have looked like. When had he last seen a picture of a whale. . . ?

Something flitted into his thoughts. About bones . . . Of large fish . . . Hadn't he just seen some pictures of bones—big bones?

With a start, he remembered. There were the pictures he had seen in the book that dealt with the history of ships. But they had been pictures about underwater wrecks. It was only that they had reminded him of the bones of big fish.

Could what he had seen when swimming across the channel have been a wreck? The wreck of an old ship—the *Swallow*?

Excited now, Tony tried to think it through. The place *was* close to the area he had seen through the captain's telescope. Yes, *Money Island*!

But how, he checked himself, could *he* have seen it when no one else had? Well, he wasn't really the first. That couple had been looking there, too. He wondered what evidence they had.

But how come—after all these years—the *Swallow* should be found now? Maybe it had been what Chris—and Grandma—had said. Big storms shift the bottoms. And there *had* been a big storm just last fall. That was it! After all these years, the *Swallow* lay exposed!

Startled by the logic of the idea, Tony sat up. It was then that he realized that some of the points around him were not just stars. They were too low. They had to be house lights. That meant land! But if he had been sailing correctly the land should be on the port—

left—side. These lights were to starboard—right. He must be going in the absolutely wrong direction!

Even as he tried to figure things out, he saw a different kind of light, a light which kept shifting, brighter then dimmer. Brighter, dimmer.

Now Tony could see a beam of light—like a white rod—come and go. The more he watched, the more he realized it must be a searchlight sweeping across the water. Maybe they were looking for him!

So quickly did he come to his knees that he almost capsized the boat. After steadying himself, he began to shout, "Hey! Here! Here I am! Help! Here!"

When there was no change in the light, he kept yelling. Now the light beam began to swing about, probing this side of him, now that, once, then twice, even momentarily blinding him. Then the light was right in his eyes. It had found him.

"Hey!" he screamed. "It's me! Over here! Help!"

He heard the roar of a motor kicking on, then sounds of a boat cutting through the water. The light remained focused on him, growing brighter and brighter. Tony kept waving his hands and yelling.

The motorboat pulled up to his side. More lights went on.

"Boy!" cried Tony. "Am I glad to see . . ."

He blinked. He could see the people in the boat. It was the couple who had been looking for the treasure.

CHAPTER *19*

The motorboat lights seemed to wrap the three of them in a cocoon of yellow light. Beyond the glow it was dark.

Tony studied the man and woman. They were both young and athletic looking. The man had close-cropped hair. His face was tan. Though he was not very big, Tony sensed he was very strong.

The woman had short hair, too, but with a band about it. She was wearing a sweatshirt with the name of some school.

"Is that you, Tony?" called the woman. "Tony Souza?"

"It's me," Tony said. "What time is it?"

"Almost midnight," the woman replied. She had a coil of rope in hand and seemed ready to throw it.

"I got lost," Tony said.

"You sure did," the man said. "You have any idea where you are?"

Tony shook his head.

"South of the Thimbles."

"South!"

"You were heading for New Haven. If you'd kept going," the woman said, "you might have reached New York City."

Tony shook his head. "My grandma must be worried."

"She and a whole bunch besides," the woman said. "The harbor master, the coast guard . . . You shouldn't be sailing alone and at night. It's not very smart."

Tony felt his cheeks burn. "I know," he admitted.

"We don't have a radio on board," the woman said. "The sooner we tow your boat back to Swallows Bay, the better."

"Thanks!"

The woman flung over the slender rope. Tony caught it.

"Can you tie it to your front cleat?" she asked.

"Think so," said Tony. He clambered forward and tied the rope down.

"Better get in with us," the man said. He hauled the rope in, drawing the *Snark* up close, then held out a hand. Tony took it and scrambled aboard the motorboat. As soon as he was on, the woman checked to see if the rope had been tied correctly to the *Snark*.

Satisfied, she let the rope play out. The *Snark* would tail behind their boat.

As Tony looked on, the man went to the dashboard. Tony was sure he saw a radio there. The man turned a key. The motor began to rumble.

Tony took a seat. He felt a touch on his arm. It was the woman. "Cold?" she asked him. "Hungry?"

"Thirsty," Tony said.

"What happened to you?" she asked, handing him a soda can. "When we heard you hadn't come back, we checked the island you were on. Not a trace."

Tony looked up. Not only was she watching him closely, the man kept looking back over his shoulder at him.

"After I . . . saw you," Tony began, feeling more and more nervous, "I went back to where I had left my boat. Except I hadn't tied her up. I think the tide came and lifted her off."

"What did you do then?" the man asked.

"I ran back to where you were, but I was too late. You had already gone."

For a moment no one said anything. Then the woman asked, "Were you spying on us?"

Tony swallowed. "I guess," he managed.

"Not the first time," she said softly. "Was it?"

Tony shook his head.

"How come?" she asked.

Tony lifted his shoulders, then let them drop. "I was . . . you know, looking for . . . the Swallows Bay treasure . . . too."

"What did you see?" the man wanted to know. "Out there."

"What do you mean?"

"When you were watching us?"

Tony looked out in the dark. "Not much," he said. He was sure the motorboat was not going as fast as it could. He felt another touch to his arm.

"You sure?" the woman asked.

"You picked up something," Tony said to her.

"What?"

"I couldn't tell."

The woman turned to the man, and Tony thought they exchanged small smiles. The man seemed to relax. "Okay," he said. The motorboat started to move faster.

"If your boat drifted off, how did you get it back?" the woman wanted to know.

"I found her on another island."

"Which one?"

"I'm not even sure if it was a different island. Maybe Money Island."

"How did you get there?"

"Swam."

The woman shook her head. "That wasn't very smart, either. What made you do that?"

"Thought I could get back to the mainland by going from one island to another."

"And?"

"Just that the current caught me. And the fog. I wasn't sure where I was."

"Since last fall's hurricane, it's gotten pretty deep around there," the woman put in. "With strong tides. You must be a good swimmer."

Tony felt a touch of pride. "It was hard," he bragged. "I really had to kick. I did get pushed off to one side. I even lost a sneaker and had to dive for it. Three times. But I did get it. That's when I saw the—" He caught himself and stopped. He wasn't fast enough.

The man abruptly cut the motor and swung about to look at Tony. The woman was staring at him, too. It had become very quiet. Once more Tony became acutely conscious of the dark that surrounded them.

"Saw what?" the man wanted to know.

Tony, alarmed, said nothing.

"Tony. . . ?" the woman urged.

"Nothing," Tony replied weakly.

The man said, "Tony, I think you better tell us what you saw."

CHAPTER 20

Tony looked from the man to the woman. There were no smiles now.

"Please," said the woman, "just tell us what you saw. We've been very patient."

Tony swallowed hard. "The . . . remains of a . . . whale."

"A *whale?*"

Tony nodded.

"In *that* channel?"

"Off to one side. I think."

"On the *far* side of Money?"

Tony shrugged.

"Tony, there are no whales around here. What made you think it was a whale?"

"Just did."

"Must have been more than that," the woman suggested.

Suddenly the man said, "Was it like the *ribs* of a whale?"

"Sort of."

"Like the ribs of a . . . ship?"

"Maybe. I don't know."

"Old?"

"Honest, I couldn't see that well. . . ."

"Tony," the man said, "was it a ship?"

Tony's voice was small. "Couldn't tell."

"But you *think* so," the woman said.

The woman and the man studied Tony, then looked at each other.

The man reached forward and turned the motor on again. "Okay, Tony. You said on the *far* side of Money Island. . . ?"

"I said I only think it was Money. I couldn't be sure."

"But it makes sense . . . " the man said softly. He turned the wheel about as the motor came to life with a low rumble. "It could have shifted. . . ."

"Where are we going?" Tony asked apprehensively.

"Swallows Bay," the woman replied.

"Eventually," the man added.

"Was it the *Swallow*?" Tony asked.

They didn't answer. Tony's heart was hammering. He kept looking from the man to the woman, wondering what they were going to do. "Did you find the payroll?" he asked.

The woman turned to look at the man. After a moment, he shrugged. Then he leaned forward, under the foredeck, and slid out a box. It was full of small things, but it was hard for Tony to see exactly what they were.

The man reached into the box and pulled out a narrow object about a foot long. It was all crusted with barnacles. He held it up.

"What is it?" Tony asked.

"Just an old bottle." The man held it out.

Tony took it, examined it, then handed it back. "The *Swallow* was a payroll ship," he said.

The man and the woman exchanged looks. The man slowly put the bottle back into the box. After a moment he said, "Tony, if that is the *Swallow*, have you any idea what she's worth?"

Tony, holding tightly to the seat on which he was sitting, shook his head.

"Could be nothing," the woman put in. "Just bottles like that."

"Or," the man added, "a million. A million bucks. Maybe more."

Tony said nothing.

It was the woman who said, "You're right about money. All our research points that way. Seems like Ezra Littlejohn was on a British ship called the *Swallow*, a payroll ship. He wasn't captain. We think he was quartermaster. Apparently, the ship got caught in

117

a storm, was driven up against the islands, and went down. Littlejohn survived. After the Revolution he came here and spent his life looking for her."

"I knew most of those things."

"How?"

"Figured it out."

Again there was only the sound of the motor.

Then Tony said, "It belongs to the state."

"Who told you that?" the man asked.

"Chris Carluci's brother. He's harbor master. At Swallows Bay."

The woman darted a look at the man, and then she said, "Tony, if you were willing to keep your discovery quiet—I mean, you know, just among ourselves, the three of us—not telling anyone else—you could get— *you*, I'm talking about, not anyone else—enough money to do whatever you liked. . . . What do you say to—ten *thousand* dollars."

"Sounds good to me," the man said, swiveling around in his seat so he could face Tony squarely. "What do you say, kid? Ten thousand dollars. All of it—*yours*."

Tony looked from the face of the man to the woman. They seemed very strong. Then he looked out over the water. The small waves, inky black, kept flicking against the boat. The stars above were still. He felt very much alone. And afraid.

"Think of all the things you could get for yourself," the woman offered. "Video games. All you could ever want. A new, better sailboat. A real one. Not a dinky toy one like that thing."

"Hey, you could even give it to your folks," the man put in. "They'd like that. Or, how about giving it to your grandmother?"

"I mean," the woman put in, her voice becoming somewhat angry, "what's the government going to do with a chest of old money?"

The man snorted. "Gobble it up."

"Look, Tony," the woman said, "we've been looking for this for a long time. Going through libraries doing research. Diving out there—a lot, a whole lot—in the cold, in the heat."

"Do I have to decide now?" Tony asked.

"Look at it this way, Tony. The moment you tell anyone else about what you saw—that's it. It'll be gone."

"What do you mean?"

"The government. Greedy politicians."

Tony asked, "What are you going to do with it?"

"Put it into a museum," the man said quickly.

"Right," the woman hastily agreed. "We want to put it on display so everybody can see it."

Tony turned around to look at the woman and the man again. He didn't believe them.

"I have to think about it," Tony managed to say.

The only sound was the motor. Tony heard the woman sigh softly.

"I think," the man said, "you should make up your mind now. Then we could get you home and a lot of people would stop worrying."

"What if . . ." Tony asked, "what if I . . . don't?"

The man said, "Look, Tony, you'd want to use the money *you* earned the way *you* wanted, wouldn't you?"

For a long while no one spoke. Tony could hear his own breath now.

Then, very dimly, Tony heard the sound of another motor. Slowly he looked around, trying to figure out where it was coming from. He turned back to the couple. He was sure they had heard it, too.

"Twenty thousand," the man snapped.

Tony stared at him.

"Whatever we find," the woman hissed. *"Half* of it!"

The beam of a high-powered searchlight swept across the water and seemed to burst upon them like an explosion, only to move off. But the next moment it returned, bathing them in glaring whiteness.

"Ahoy!" came a cry.

"Don't be an idiot, Tony . . ." Tony heard the man whisper sharply. "Just think of all that money!"

Tony leaped up. "Here we are!" he cried out. *"Here!"* Out in the water a motor roared toward them.

In moments the harbor master's motorboat pulled alongside. Steve was behind the wheel. Chris was there. So was Grandma.

"Tony!" Chris called. "Is everything okay?"

"The *Swallow*," Tony called. "It's been found! And they've been taking things from her!"

CHAPTER 21

It was almost two o'clock in the morning. Tony was sitting at the kitchen table in his grandma's house. The once-full pile of lemon cookies on the plate had been reduced to crumbs.

Next to Tony sat his grandma, her hands clasped before her. She was tired, but not prepared to go to bed. Next to her was Chris. The other person was Chris's brother, Steve, the harbor master.

". . . and that's the way it happened," Tony said, finishing his story. He had told it all, from the time he had made up his mind to go into the Thimbles, to the moment they plucked him out of the couple's motorboat.

"Do you think you can lead us out to where you saw the wreck?" Steve asked.

"I'm pretty sure I can," Tony answered. "I think it's right off Money Island."

"Figures," Chris said with a wry grin.

"There's another way to find it," Tony said. He reached into a pocket and held out his hand. The small lens rested in his palm.

"What's that?"

"A lens for Littlejohn's spyglass. I found it in Grandpa's ship model. If you look through his spyglass—the one the statue's holding—you'll see. I think it's aimed right at Money Island."

Chris and Steve laughed.

Grandma shook her head. "I think you were very lucky. That's what I think. I'll tell you, you did a lot of stupid things."

Tony looked around sheepishly. He could tell Chris and her brother agreed.

"I know," he said.

The harbor master said, "Do you think those two—that man and the woman—would have done anything to you if we hadn't come up then?"

Tony looked around. "I don't know. So far, all they were doing was offering me lots of money if I didn't tell about the wreck."

"A bribe," Chris said.

"How much?" Grandma wanted to know.

Tony grinned. "They started at ten thousand," he said. "Then it went up to twenty, and then to half of whatever they found. How much do you think is there?" he asked.

Chris lifted up two empty hands. "No telling," she

said. "It could be a lot. But don't be surprised if it's nothing."

"But," put in her brother, "depending on what condition that old wreck is in, that alone could have tremendous value for historical research. That's the main reason the state makes sure those wrecks aren't touched."

Tony grew thoughtful.

Grandma reached across to touch his arm. "Second thoughts? All that money. Is that what you're thinking?"

"Well . . ."

"Speak what you're thinking," Grandma urged.

"If I ask my folks—and they say yes—can I stay the rest of the summer?"

Grandma looked very solemn. "Tony, I don't think you'll find any more treasures."

"I know. But—" Suddenly Tony laughed and said, *"Espero que—"*

Grandma grinned broadly and finished the sentence. *"Vece alcance vento dos seus desejos."*

"What's that mean?" Chris wanted to know.

"He'd rather catch the wind," Grandma said.

"Yeah," Tony said, "you get to keep it."